HOME, FAMILY & EVERYDAY LIFE
through the ages

Series Editor Dr. John Haywood

LORENZ BOOKS

First published by Lorenz Books in 2001

© Anness Publishing Limited 2001

Published in the USA by Lorenz Books,
Anness Publishing Inc.,
27 West 20th Street,
New York
NY10011

Lorenz Books is an imprint of Anness Publishing Inc.

www.lorenzbooks.com

All rights reserved. No part of this publication may be reproduced, stored in a retrieval system, or transmitted in any way or by any means, electronic, mechanical, photocopying, recording, or otherwise, without the prior written permission of the copyright holder.

Publisher Joanna Lorenz
Managing Editor, Children's Books Gilly Cameron Cooper
Project Editor Rasha Elsaeed
Editorial Reader Jonathan Marshall
"From Shelters to Homes" Introduction by Fiona Macdonald
Authors Daud Ali, Jen Green, Charlotte Hurdman, Fiona Macdonald, Lorna Oakes, Philip Steele, Michael Stotter, Richard Tames
Consultants Nick Allen, Cherry Alexander, Clara Bezanilla, Felicity Cobbing, Penny Dransart, Jenny Hall, Dr. John Haywood, Dr. Robin Holgate, Michael Johnson, Lloyd Laing, Jessie Lim, Heidi Potter, Louise Schofield, Leslie Webster,
Designers Simon Borrough, Matthew Cook, Joyce Mason, Caroline Reeves, Margaret Sadler, Alison Walker, Stuart Watkinson at Ideas Into Print, Sarah Williams
Special Photography John Freeman
Stylists Konika Shakar, Thomasina Smith, Melanie Williams

Previously published as part of the *Step Into* series in 14 separate volumes:
Ancient Egypt, Ancient Greece, Ancient India, Ancient Japan, Arctic World, Aztec & Maya Worlds, Celtic World, Chinese Empire, Inca World, Mesopotamia, North American Indians, Roman Empire, Viking World, The Stone Age.

PICTURE CREDITS
b=bottom, t=top, c=centre, l=left, r=right

Lesley & Roy Adkins Picture Library: 35bl; AKG: 10b, 11tl, 18c, 19tl, 44bl; B & C Alexander: title page 48cl, 49cl & 49tr, 50cl, 51c, 52cl & 52cr, 53tr & 53cl; The Ancient Art & Architecture Collection Ltd: 12, 13bl, 14b, 15bc, 23br, 28tr, 32tr & 32bl, 35bl, 43tr; Andes Press Agency: 61bl; GDR Barnett Images: 54tl; The Bodleian Library: 56bl, 57bl; A-Z Botanical Collection Ltd: 33r; Bildarchiv Preussischer Kulturbesitz: 10t, 11br; The Bridgeman Art Library: 43l; The British Museum: 13tr, 14t, 15tr, 32br, 34l; Bulloz: 10m; Jean-Loup Charmet: 61t & 61br; Peter Clayton: 28cl, 29tr, 30l; Corbis: 14tr, 16tr, 18tl, 19cl, 44br, 45cl, 46c, 51tl; Sue Cunningham Photographic: 59tl & 59tr; C M Dixon: front cover, 8tl & 8b, 9bl & 9br, 13tl, 15tl, 27cl, 34r, 36tl & 36c, 37tr & 37c, 38cr, 39tl & 39cl, 41tr, 43tl, 46cl & 47tr, 47cl, 56tl; E T Archive: 3, 7tc, 22tr & 22bl, 23bl, 24tr, 25tr, 26tl, 27tr, 40bl, 43br, 54tr; Mary Evans Picture Library: 22br, 53tl, 57br; Werner Forman Archive: 24cr, 33tl, 41tl, 57tr, 60t & 60br; Robert Harding: 11tr, 14b, 15bl, 16b, 17bl, 41bl, 43c; MacQuitty Collections: 25cl; Michael Holford: 28tl, 29rl, 33bl; National Museum of Scotland: 37cl; Peter Newark: 44tr, 45tl, 47tl & 47tr; NHPA: 27c; Planet Earth: 48tl, 50tl, 58b; South American Photo Library: 26bl, 54cl, 58t, 60bl; Statens Historic Museum: 42tr; Tony Stone: 51tr; Visual Arts Library: 23tr, 26tl; Keith Welch: 37tl; York University Trust: 40tr, 41br, 42b; ZEFA: 21tr

10 9 8 7 6 5 4 3 2 1

CONTENTS

From Shelters to Homes ...4

Stone Age Villages ...8

Family Life in Mesopotamia ...10

Egyptian Houses and Gardens ...12

Egyptian Food ...14

Rich and Poor in India ...16

Eating in India ...18

Chinese Homes in Harmony ...20

Traditional Life in China ...22

Food and Diet in China ...24

Family Life in Japan ...26

Growing Up in Greece ...28

Roman Houses ...30

Family Occasions in Rome ...32

Roman Education 34

Life on a Celtic Farm 36

Celtic Food and Drink 38

Viking Family Life 40

Viking Women 42

North American Homes 44

Tribal Family Roles 46

Cold-Climate Homes 48

Arctic Seasonal Camps.....................50

Arctic Children 52

Aztec and Mayan Homes.................54

Mesoamerican Families 56

An Incan House 58

Married Life in Incan Times 60

Glossary 62

Index 64

KEY
Look for the patterns used throughout this book, there is one for each culture

- The Stone Age
- Mesopotamia
- Ancient Egypt
- India
- China
- Japan
- Ancient Greece
- Roman Empire
- The Celts
- The Vikings
- North American Indians
- The Arctic
- Aztec & Maya
- Inca Empire

From Shelters to Homes

Everyone needs somewhere to live. All over the world, people from different civilizations have built many kinds of homes. From the simplest prehistoric cave-shelters, to the most splendid palaces in Mughal India, a home serves many purposes that are common in all cultures. They provided protection from cold and damp, shade from the hot sun, and comfortable refuge for sleeping, preparing food, raising a family, and entertaining guests.

The layout and construction of houses varied widely. Homes were designed to provide maximum comfort in the local climate, and to withstand local environmental hazards, such as storms, floods, earthquakes, and heavy snow. In northern Europe, the Vikings built houses with thick thatched roofs for insulation from the cold. In Japan, an earthquake zone, lightweight paper screens were used as inner walls in the construction of houses. If these collapsed, they

Round, early farming huts, such as this one, whose remains were found in Banpo in China, date from 6000 B.C. They had wooden frames, plastered walls, and a hole to let out smoke.

Longhouses were alternatives to the round house. These were often found in Europe, and north and south America. Thatch made from reeds from a nearby river lasted longer than straw.

Timeline 10,000–200 B.C.

10,000 B.C. People around the world live as nomads, moving from place to place, hunting animals and gathering wild foods. They shelter in strong, solid houses, made of wood, stone, or snow in winter, but travel around, living in tents in summer. Seminomadic lifestyle continues until the 1900s in places such as arctic Russia.

Inside an igloo home of the Arctic Inuit people

10,000 B.C. People living in north and south America develop homes according to the local environment. Some are simple shelters of branches and leaves; others include earth lodges, longhouses made of woven saplings, buffalo-skin tipis, and mud-brick pueblo apartments.

8000–7000 B.C. The world's first settled farming villages are built in the Middle East.

4500 B.C. European farmers build villages of longhouses.

3100–30 B.C. The peak of ancient Egyptian civilization. Egyptians live in houses made of sun-dried mud brick.

European longhouse village

800 B.C.–A.D. 100 The Celts in central and northwestern Europe live as

10,000 B.C.   4500 B.C.   3000 B.C.

4   INTRODUCTION

would not harm people and cause much damage.

The materials used to construct a house also shaped its design. Most homes were built using local resources that were easily available. In many countries, including Aztec Mexico and ancient Egypt, mud and clay were shaped into bricks and dried in the sun. Elsewhere, homes were made from wood, stone, and dried grass. Fine stone and timber were rare, and it was difficult to carry them long distances, so they were expensive. The materials used and the size of homes depended on the wealth of the owner. Houses of the wealthy were large and luxurious, with many spacious rooms. Among the poor, all family members might share a simple room that combined as sleeping and living space.

Houses were built on stilts in the marshy regions of Japan, where rice was cultivated in wet paddy fields.

Tipis made of animal skins were held up with wooden poles, and they served as a short-term shelter for Native American peoples.

Most homes were built as permanent shelters, but in some environments, they were designed to fulfill temporary needs. Nomads were people who moved from place to place, hunting animals and gathering wild plants for food. They built homes that were designed to be easily packed away and moved several times a year. Native American hunters on the Great Plains of North America made tipis of buffalo skin. Inuit hunters in the Arctic built shelters from blocks of snow, called igloos,

---

farmers, building large roundhouses of wattle-and-daub, thatched with straw. They also build fortified towns as centers of trade.

600 B.C. Wealthy families in India build houses of brick and stone. They are painted different colors, according to caste (social status).

600–200 B.C. Ancient Greek families live in houses made of stone or mud bricks. They have separate, private quarters for women, and a dining room for entertaining, used only by men of the family.

***c*. 300 B.C.–A.D. 300** Wealthy Roman families build splendid houses. Town houses were often built around a small enclosed garden, or a courtyard called an atrium. Country houses had elegant rooms for entertaining, plus barracks where slaves and farmworkers could sleep.

300 B.C. In Central America, the Maya build new cities surrounded by fields and farms. Mayan families live in simple homes, with wood or mud walls and thatched roofs.

A wealthy Roman family home.

300 B.C.   400 B.C.   300 B.C.   A.D. 200

FROM SHELTERS TO HOMES   5

to live in during the long winter months.

For many people, homes were also places of work. From the time when humans first began to live together in families, women worked at home, caring for babies and young children. In most cultures, women did the cooking and produced household textiles, such as blankets and clothes, for their families. Archaeologists have found children's toys, cooking pots, and the remains of weaving looms in family homes from places as diverse as India and Incan Peru. Men, who made their living as farmers and craftspeople, also worked at home, with other family members helping them. Teamwork was essential for survival. Children worked alongside their parents, learning the skills they would need in adult life. School was only provided for children from wealthy families, as in China and imperial Rome.

Backstrap looms started to be used as early as 2500 B.C. by the people who lived in the Andes mountains of Peru.

All these family and working needs were reflected in house designs. Craft workshops, rooms to display finished goods, and shelters for farm animals often formed part of the family home. Cultural values also influenced housing. In ancient Greece, homes had private rooms where women lived, out of the sight of

Homelife in early Middle Eastern farming villages was a cluster of activity. People often shared their house with the animals. Everyone in the family had a role to play.

Timeline 200 B.C.–A.D. 1500

206 B.C.–A.D. 220 The Han dynasty rules China. Large, extended families live in courtyard homes, with many different rooms surrounded by strong walls, and guarded by gates and a watchtower.

A.D. 1–1000 The Dorset people of the North American Arctic live as nomad hunters in the summer and in snow-house villages during the winter.

A Chinese Han dynasty house

A.D. 700–1100 The Vikings from Scandinavia build new settlements in many European lands, also in Iceland, Greenland, and North America. Viking homes are built to withstand the cold, with thick roofs and walls. Depending on the site, they are built from stone, wood and thatch, or turf.

710 The Nara empire comes to power in Japan. They built a splendid new capital city at Nara.

200 B.C.   A.D. 100   700   800

nonfamily men. Almost everywhere, people liked to decorate their houses, sometimes in bright colors and patterns, and to furnish them with comfortable bedding, seating, and floor-coverings. Some of these decorations had a meaning, with the aim of protecting a house or watching over those who lived there. Chinese families often displayed a picture of the kitchen god, who monitored their behavior. Some Native Americans put up tall totem poles outside their homes, carved with images of ancestor spirits, to guard the families.

This book charts the development of domestic history in various cultures in turn. It focuses on aspects of everyday life that are common to major civilizations, such as family, childhood, education, housing, and food. You will be able to see how these themes evolved and compare how people's lives varied with local environments around the world.

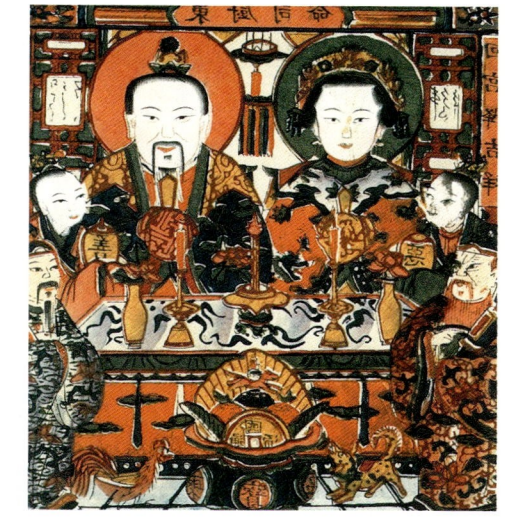

In every Chinese kitchen, a new paper picture of the kitchen god and his wife was put up on New Year's Day.

An Aztec couple sit by the fire, while their meal is being cooked. Their colorful clothes and braided hair indicate that they are people of rank.

Wooden totem poles outside Native American homes kept a record of the family histories of the people living inside.

1000–1325 The Aztec people of Central America leave their homeland in the north of Mexico, and travel south in search of a better place to live. They settle in the central valley of Mexico and build a new capital city Tenochtitlan. It soon grows into one of the largest cities in the world.

1000–1600 The Thule people of the North American Arctic live in huts made of stone and turf.

Inca man and woman gather straw for thatch

*c.*1300–1536 The Inca Empire is powerful in Peru. The Incas are expert builders, of stone temples, palaces, and city walls, without using metal tools. Ordinary families live in small stone houses, thatched with straw.

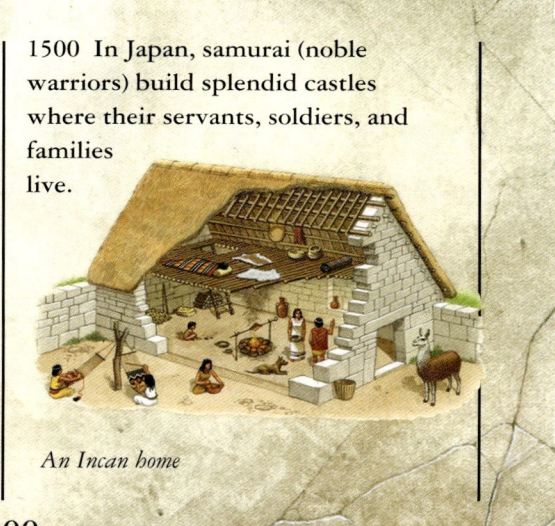

1500 In Japan, samurai (noble warriors) build splendid castles where their servants, soldiers, and families live.

An Incan home

1000   1300   1500

FROM SHELTERS TO HOMES   7

Stone Age Villages

PRIMITIVE HUMANS hunted wild animals, caught fish, and gathered berries and plants to eat. When people took up farming as a way of life, it meant that they had to stay in the same place for a long time. Some farmers practiced slash and burn. This means that they cleared the land, but moved after a few years, when their crops had exhausted the soil. Elsewhere, early farming settlements grew into villages five to ten times bigger than earlier hunter-gatherer camps. At first, the farmers still hunted animals, but soon their herds and crops supplied most of their needs. They lived in villages of rectangular or circular one-story houses made from stone, mud brick, or timber and thatch. Houses were connected by narrow lanes and courtyards. Most villages lay near well-watered, easily worked land. By using irrigation and crop rotation, later farmers were able to stay in one place for a long time.

INSIDE A LONGHOUSE
The inside of a longhouse was a place of work, and it also provided shelter for the family and their animals. Around the hearth of this reconstructed house are baskets woven from reeds and skins laid out the floor. Tools are stored around the walls.

A LONGHOUSE
This is a reconstruction of a typical longhouse in an early farming village in Europe. The village dates from around 4500 B.C.

8   THE STONE AGE   120,000 B.C.–2000 B.C.

A Town House

This picture shows how a house at Çatal Hüyük in Turkey may have looked. The walls were made of mud brick, with a roof made from poles covered with reeds and mud. All the houses were joined together, with no streets in between. People got around by climbing over the rooftops, entering their homes by a ladder through the roof.

The main room of each house had raised areas for sitting and sleeping. More than a thousand houses were packed together like this one at Çatal Hüyük.

The Oven

Many houses contained ovens or kilns, used for baking bread and firing pottery. A kiln allowed higher temperatures to be reached than an open hearth, and therefore produced better pottery. Each village probably made its own pottery.

Stone Walls

These are the remains of the walls of a house in an early farming village in Jordan. It was built around 7000 B.C. The walls are made from stone collected from the local area. The first farming towns and villages appeared in the Near East. Most were built from mud brick, and over hundreds of years, such settlements were often rebuilt many times on the same site.

STONE AGE VILLAGES 9

Family Life in Mesopotamia

LIFE WAS HARD for ordinary families in Mesopotamia. Many babies and young children died from disease, or because of poor maternity care. Boys from poorer families did not go to school, but worked with their fathers, who taught them their trades. Girls stayed at home with their mothers—they learned how to keep house and helped to take care of the younger children. Some of the details of family life are described in ancient clay tablets. In one tablet, a boy rudely tells his mother to hurry up and make his lunch. In another one, a boy is scared of what his father will say when he sees his bad school report.

In some ways, Mesopotamian society was quite modern. The law said that women could own property and get a divorce. However, if a woman was unable to have a baby for any reason, she had to agree to her husband taking a second wife. The second wife and her children had rights, too. They remained part of the household, even if the first wife had a child eventually.

MOTHERHOOD
Having lots of healthy children, especially sons, was very important, because families needed children to grow up and work for them. Most women stayed at home to take care of their families. Women did not usually go out to work, although some had jobs as priestesses. Some priestesses were single, but others were married women.

HOUSEHOLD GOODS
Pottery was used in Mesopotamian homes from the time of the first villages. At first it was handmade, but later, a potter's wheel was used. This clay jug may have been based on one made of metal. Tools and utensils were made of stone or metal. There was not much furniture in a Mesopotamian house—just mud brick benches for sitting or sleeping on. There may have been rugs and cushions to make the homes more comfortable, but none have survived.

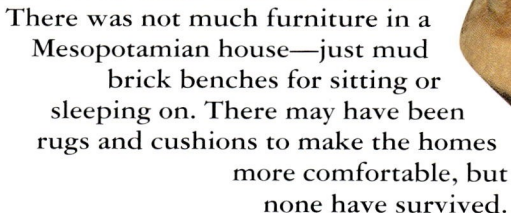

MODEL HOUSE
From models such as this one, we know that homes in Mesopotamia were similar to village houses in modern Iraq. They were built from mud brick and were usually rectangular, with rooms around a central courtyard. Doors and windows were small to keep the house warm in the cold winters and cool during the hot summers. Flat roofs, which were reached by stairs from the central court, could be used as extra rooms in the summer.

MESOPOTAMIAN FASHIONS

A statue of a worshipper found in a temple shows the dress of a Sumerian woman. Dresses were made from sheepskin, also with a sheepskin shawl, or from woolen cloth. One shoulder was left bare. Some women, who may have been priestesses, wore tall, elaborate hats like this one. Later fashions included long, fringed garments. Sumerian men wore sheepskin kilts, and men in the Assyrian and Babylonian Empires wore long, woolen tunics. Both men and women wore jewelery.

EARNING A LIVING

Most families in ancient Mesopotamia depended on agriculture for a living, just as many people in the Middle East do today. Farmers rented their land from bigger landowners, such as important officials, kings, and temples, and had to give part of what they produced in taxes. Many townspeople had jobs in the local government or worked in the textile and metalwork industries.

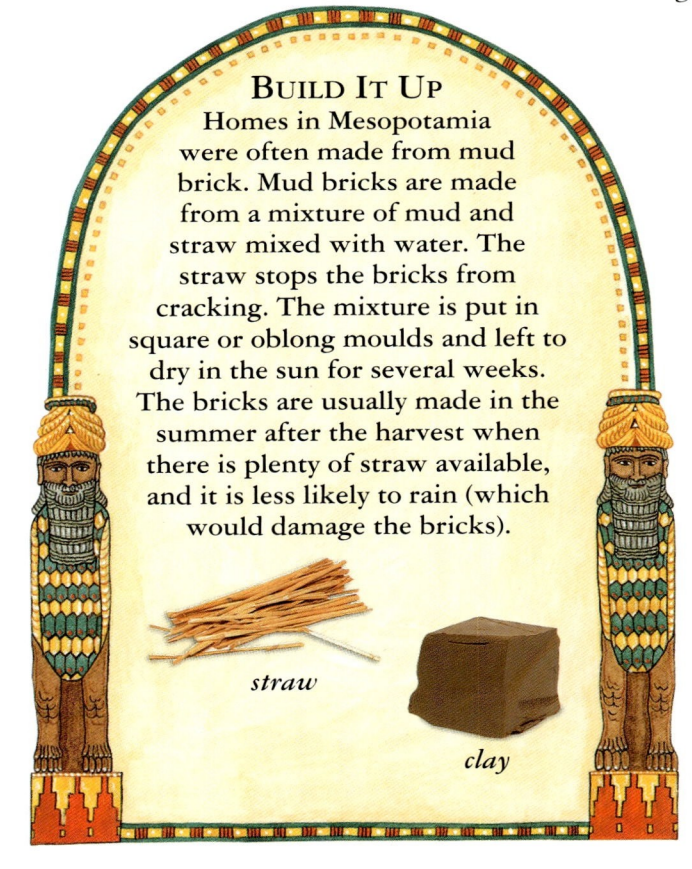

BUILD IT UP

Homes in Mesopotamia were often made from mud brick. Mud bricks are made from a mixture of mud and straw mixed with water. The straw stops the bricks from cracking. The mixture is put in square or oblong moulds and left to dry in the sun for several weeks. The bricks are usually made in the summer after the harvest when there is plenty of straw available, and it is less likely to rain (which would damage the bricks).

straw

clay

GONE FISHING

There were lots of fish in the rivers and fishponds of ancient Iraq, and fish seem to have been an important part of people's diet. Fishbones were found at Eridu, in the south of Sumer, in the oldest level of the temple. Perhaps fish were offered to the water god Enki as an offering. (He is the god with streams of water containing fish springing out of his shoulders.) Some of the carved reliefs from the Assyrian palaces give us rare glimpses into everyday life that include little scenes of men going fishing.

Egyptian Houses and Gardens

THE GREAT CITIES of ancient Egypt, such as Memphis and Thebes, were built along the banks of the River Nile. Small towns grew up haphazardly around them. Special workmen's towns, such as Deir el-Medina, were set up around major burial sites and temples to help with building work.

Egyptian towns were defended by thick walls, and the streets were planned on a grid pattern. The straight dirt roads had a stone drainage channel, or gutter, running down the middle. Parts of the town housed important officials, and other parts were home to craftspeople and poor laborers.

Only temples were built to last—they were made of stone. Mud brick was used to construct all other buildings, from royal palaces to workers' dwellings. Most Egyptian homes had roofs supported with palm logs, and floors made of packed earth. In the homes of wealthier Egyptians, walls were sometimes plastered and painted. The rooms of their houses included bedrooms, living rooms, kitchens in thatched courtyards, and workshops. Homes were furnished with beds, chairs, stools, and benches. In the cool of the evenings, people would sit on the flat roofs, or walk and talk in shady gardens.

THE GARDEN OF NAKHT
The royal scribe Nakht and his wife Tjiui take an evening stroll through their garden. Trees and shrubs surround a peaceful pool. Egyptian gardens included date palms, pomegranates, grape vines, scarlet poppies, and blue and pink lotus flowers. Artists in ancient Egypt showed objects in the same picture from different angles, so the trees around Nakht's pool are flattened out.

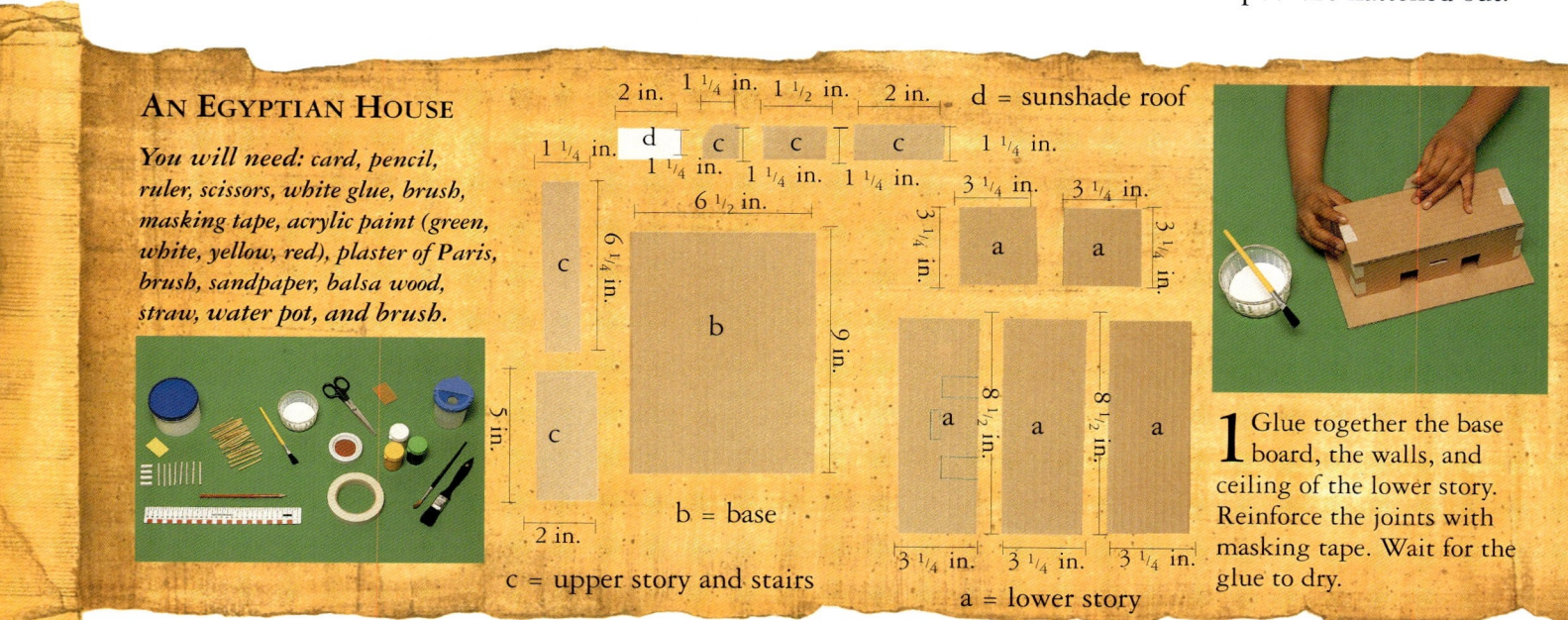

AN EGYPTIAN HOUSE

You will need: card, pencil, ruler, scissors, white glue, brush, masking tape, acrylic paint (green, white, yellow, red), plaster of Paris, brush, sandpaper, balsa wood, straw, water pot, and brush.

d = sunshade roof
b = base
c = upper story and stairs
a = lower story

1 Glue together the base board, the walls, and ceiling of the lower story. Reinforce the joints with masking tape. Wait for the glue to dry.

12 ANCIENT EGYPT 6000 B.C.–50 B.C.

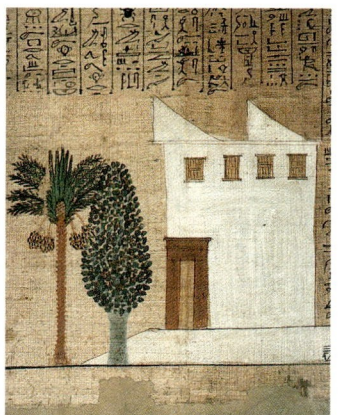

ABOVE THE FLOODS
The homes of wealthy people were often built on platforms to stop damp from passing through the mud brick walls. This also raised it above the level of any possible flood damage.

SOUL HOUSES
Pottery models give us a good idea of how the homes of poorer Egyptians looked. During the Middle Kingdom (2050–1786 B.C.), these soul houses were left as tomb offerings. The Egyptians placed food in the courtyard of the house, to feed the person's soul after death.

NILE SOILS
The Egyptians built their homes from mud bricks that were made from the thick clay soil left behind by the Nile floods. The clay was taken to the brickyard and mixed with water, pebbles, and chopped straw. Mud bricks are still used for building houses in Egypt today, and are made in the same way.

straw *mud*

BRICK MAKING
A group of laborers make bricks. First, mud was collected in leather buckets and taken to the building site. There, it was mixed with straw and pebbles. Finally, the mixture was put into a mold. At this stage, bricks were sometimes stamped with the name of the pharaoh or the building for which they were made. They were then left to dry in the hot sunshine for several days, before being transported in a sling.

Egyptian houses had a large main room that opened directly onto the street. In many homes, stairs led up to the roof. People would often sleep there during very hot weather.

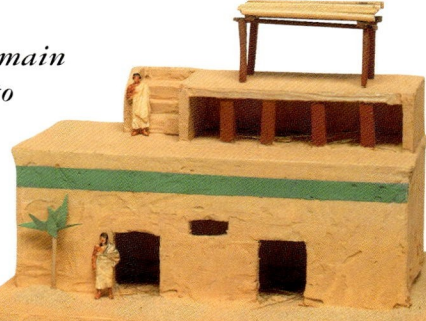

2 Now glue together the top story and stairs. Again, use masking tape to reinforce the joints. When the top story is dry, glue it to the lower story.

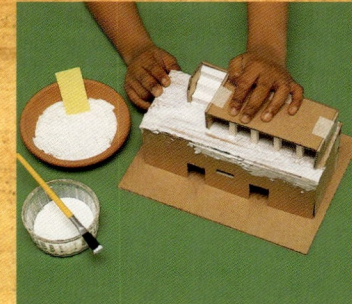

3 Glue the balsa pillars to the front of the top story. When the house is dry, cover it in wet paste of plaster of Paris. Paint the pillars red or a color of your choice.

4 Paint the whole building a dried mud color. Next, paint a green strip along the side. Use masking tape to make straight edges. Sand any rough edges.

5 Now make a shelter for the rooftop. Use four balsa struts as supports. The roof can be made from card glued with straw. Glue the shelter into place.

EGYPTIAN HOUSES AND GARDENS

Egyptian Food

LABORERS IN ANCIENT Egypt were often paid in food. They ate bread, onions, and salted fish, washed down with a sweet, grainy beer. Flour was often gritty, and the teeth of many mummified bodies show signs of severe wear and tear. Dough was kneaded with the feet or by hand, and pastry cooks produced all kinds of cakes and loaves.

A big banquet for a pharaoh was a grand affair, with guests dressed in their finest clothes. A royal menu might include roast goose or stewed beef, kidneys, wild duck, or tender gazelle. For religious reasons, lamb was not eaten, and in some regions certain types of fish were also forbidden. Vegetables such as leeks were stewed with milk and cheese. Egyptian cooks were experts at stewing, roasting, and baking.

Red and white wines were served at banquets. They were stored in pottery jars marked with their year and their vineyard, just like the labels on modern wine bottles.

BEAUTIFUL BOWLS
Dishes and bowls were often made of faience, a glassy pottery. The usual colors for this attractive tableware was blue-green and turquoise.

A FEAST FIT FOR A KING
New Kingdom (1550–1070 B.C.) noblewomen exchange gossip at a dinner party. They show off their jewelry and best clothes. Egyptians loved wining and dining. They would be entertained by musicians, dancers, and acrobats during the feast.

MAKE A PASTRY

You will need: $3/4$ *cip + 1 tbsp. stoneground flour,* $1/2$ *tsp. salt, 1 tsp. baking powder,* $3/4$ *stick butter, 4 tbsp. honey, 3 tbsp. milk, caraway seeds, bowl, wooden spoon, baking tray.*

1 Begin by mixing together the flour, salt, and baking powder in the bowl. Next, chop up the butter and add it to the dry ingredients.

2 Using your fingers, rub the butter into the flour, as shown. Your dough should look like fine breadcrumbs when you have finished.

3 Now add $2/3$ of your honey. Mix it in with the dough. This will sweeten your pastries. The ancient Egyptians did not have sugar.

14 ANCIENT EGYPT 6000 B.C.–50 B.C.

WOMAN MAKING BEER
This wooden tomb model of a woman making beer dates back to 2400 B.C. Beer was made by mashing barley bread in water. When the mixture fermented and became alcoholic, the liquid was strained into a wooden tub. There were various types of beer, but all were very popular. It was said that the god Osiris had brought beer to the land of Egypt.

DRINKING VESSEL
Beautiful faience cups such as this one could have been used to drink wine, water, and beer. It is decorated with a pattern of lotus flowers.

DESERT DESSERTS
A meal in ancient Egypt was often completed with nuts, such as almonds, and sweet fruits: juicy figs, dates, grapes, pomegranates, and melons. Sugar was still unknown, so honey was used to sweeten cakes and pastries.

pomegranates

dates

PALACE BAKERY
Whole teams of model cooks and bakers were left in some tombs. This was so that a pharaoh could order them to put on a good banquet to entertain his guests in the other world. Models are shown sifting, mixing, and kneading flour, and also making pastries. Most of our knowledge about Egyptian food and cooking comes from the food boxes and offerings left in tombs.

Egyptian pastries were often shaped in spirals like these. Other popular shapes were rings, like doughnuts, and pyramids. Some were shaped like crocodiles!

4 Add the milk and stir the dough until it is smooth. Roll your dough into a ball, and place it on a floured board or surface. Divide the dough into three.

5 Roll the dough into long strips, as shown. Take a strip and coil it into a spiral to make one pastry. Make the other pastries in the same way.

6 Now sprinkle each pastry with caraway seeds and place them all on a greased baking tray. Complete by glazing the pastries carefully with a little extra honey.

7 Ask an adult to bake them in an oven at 350°F for 20 minutes. When they are ready, take them out and leave on a baking rack to cool.

EGYPTIAN FOOD

Rich and Poor in India

Houses in India differed according to social class. Poor people made their homes out of mud, clay, and thatch. Materials such as these do not last long, so few of these houses have survived. By about 600 B.C., wealthier people were building homes made of brick and stone. It is thought that people's caste (class) determined not only the part of a town or city that they lived in, but also what color they painted their homes. The Brahmins (priests caste) of Jodhpur in Rajasthan, for example, painted their houses blue.

A wealthy man's house of about A.D. 400 had a courtyard and an outer room where guests were entertained. Behind this were the inner rooms where the women of the house stayed and where food was cooked. Beyond the house itself, there were often gardens and fountains surrounded by an outside wall. Homes like this stayed much the same in design over many centuries.

Royal palaces were more elaborate. They had many courtyards, and enclosures surrounded by numerous walls. These were to protect the king from beggars and servants who might make a nuisance of themselves. Unlike ordinary homes, palaces changed in design with each new wave of rulers.

Decorated doorstep
Pictures in chalk and rice powder were drawn on the doorsteps of houses. Over time, they came to signify prosperity and good luck. Making such drawings was one of 64 forms of art that a cultured person was expected to be able to do.

birdcage

mango leaves hung for good luck

water trough

courtyard

Mountain Homes
These modern mountain homes made from mud and thatch continue a tradition that is thousands of years old. Unlike valley homes, they have to be well insulated for protection against the colder climate.

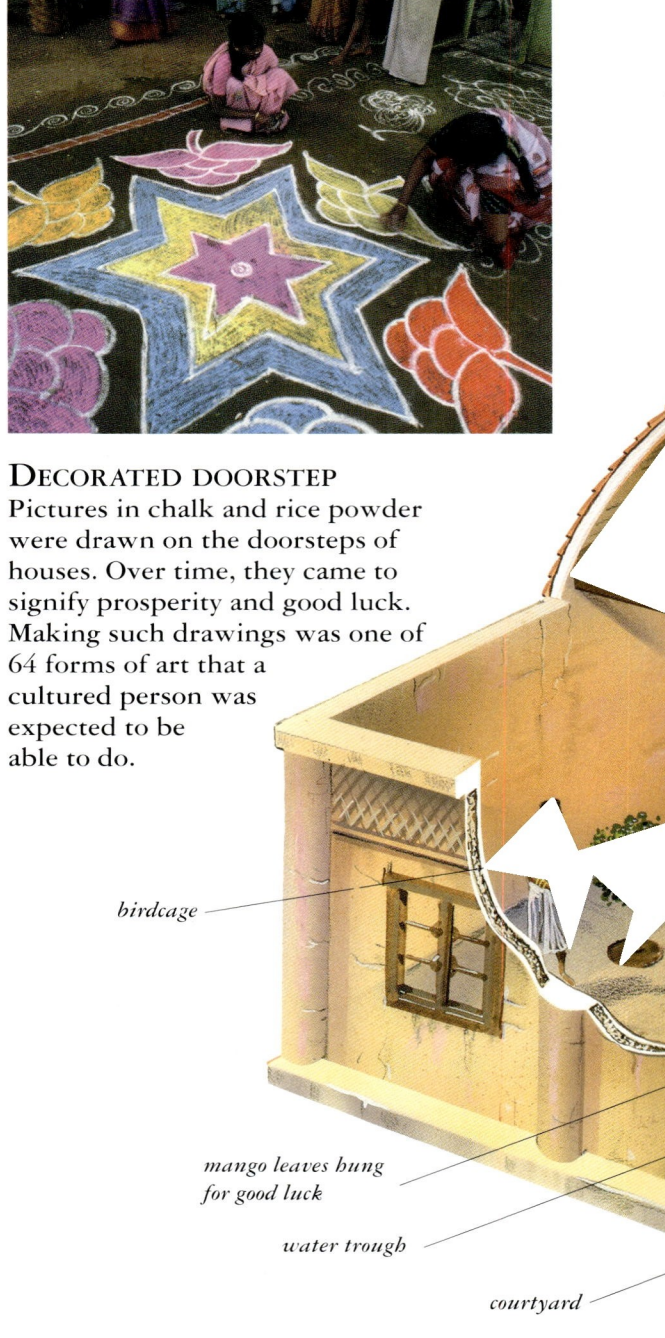

The Good Life
Life in a rich man's household was divided between the inner area, where he slept and ate, and the outer regions, dominated by a courtyard where he entertained friends, read, listened to music, and strolled in the garden. Here, salons (groups) of men would meet to discuss life and politics.

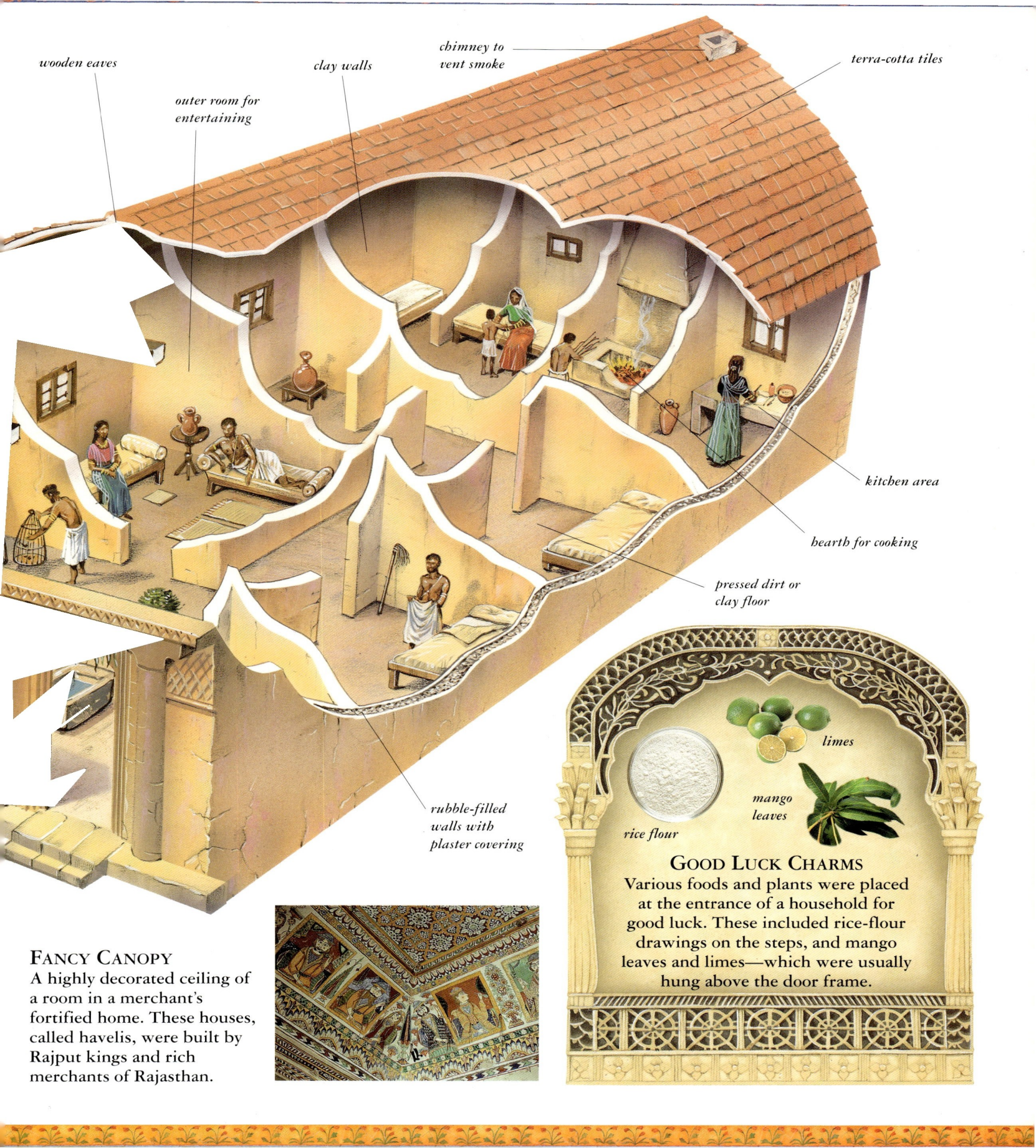

wooden eaves · outer room for entertaining · clay walls · chimney to vent smoke · terra-cotta tiles · kitchen area · hearth for cooking · pressed dirt or clay floor · rubble-filled walls with plaster covering

FANCY CANOPY
A highly decorated ceiling of a room in a merchant's fortified home. These houses, called havelis, were built by Rajput kings and rich merchants of Rajasthan.

limes · mango leaves · rice flour

GOOD LUCK CHARMS
Various foods and plants were placed at the entrance of a household for good luck. These included rice-flour drawings on the steps, and mango leaves and limes—which were usually hung above the door frame.

Eating in India

PEOPLE'S STAPLE (BASIC) FOODS in the ancient world depended on what they could grow. In the wetter areas of eastern, western, southern, and central India, rice was the staple diet. In the drier areas of the north and northwest, people grew wheat and made it into different kinds of breads.

Apart from these staple foods, people's diets depended on their religion. Buddhists thought that killing animals was wrong, so they were vegetarians. Most Hindus, particularly the upper castes, became vegetarian, too. Because they believed that the cow was holy, eating beef became taboo (forbidden). When Islam arrived, it brought with it a new set of rules. Muslims are forbidden to eat pork, although they do eat other meat.

The Indians used a lot of spices in cooking, in order to add flavor and to disguise the taste of rotten meat. Ginger, garlic, turmeric, cinnamon, and cumin were used from early times. Chilis were only introduced from the Americas after the 1500s.

CELESTIAL FRUITS
A heavenly damsel offers fruits in this stucco painting from Sri Lanka. From earliest times, Indians ate with their hands rather than with implements. Even so, there were rules to be followed. Generally, they could only eat with the right hand, taking care only to use their fingers.

EVENING DELIGHTS
A princess enjoys an evening party in the garden. She listens to music by candlelight, and is served drinks, sweets, and other foods.

MAKE A CHICKPEA CURRY
You will need: knife, a small onion, 2 tsbp. vegetable oil, wok or frying pan, wooden spoon, 1 1/2 in. piece fresh ginger root, 2 cloves garlic, 1/4 tsp. turmeric, 1 lb. tomatoes, 1/2 lb. cooked chickpeas, salt and pepper, 2 tbsp. finely chopped fresh coriander, plus coriander leaves to garnish, 2 tsp. garam masala, a lime.

1 Chop the onion finely. Heat the vegetable oil in a wok. Fry the onion in the oil for two to three minutes, until it is soft. Ask an adult to help you.

2 Chop the ginger finely and add to the pan. Chop the garlic clove and add it, along with the turmeric. Cook gently for another half a minute.

A Rich Banquet

Babur, the founder of the Mughal Empire in India in A.D. 1526, enjoys a banquet of roast duck in Herat, Persia. Under the Mughals, a cuisine known as Mughlai developed. It became famous for its rich and sophisticated flavors.

Three Essential Spices

turmeric

black mustard seeds

cardamom

Many spices are used in Indian dishes. Turmeric is ground from a root to give food an earthy flavor and yellow color. Black mustard seed has a smoky, bitter taste. Cardamom—a favorite in northern India—gives a musky, sugary flavor that is suitable for both sweet and savory dishes.

Leaf Plate

In southern India, banana leaves were (and are still) used as plates for serving and eating food. Southern Indian food uses more coconut than the north, and rice flour is used in several dishes.

Daily Bread

Indians eat a variety of baked, griddled, and fried breads, such as these parathas. In much of northern and western India, the staple food is wheat, which is baked into unleavened (flat) breads.

Chickpeas are a popular ingredient in Indian cooking. They have been grown in India for thousands of years.

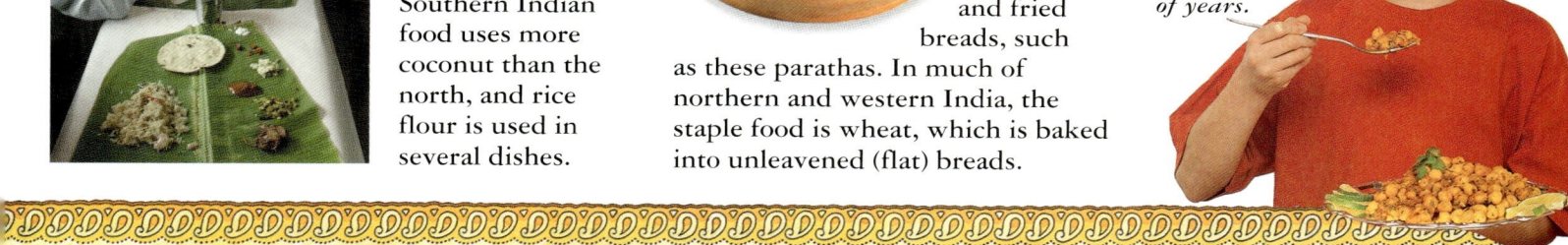

3 Peel the tomatoes, cut them in half, and remove the seeds. Then chop them roughly and add them to the onion, garlic, and spice mixture.

4 Add the chickpeas. Bring to a boil, then simmer gently for 10–15 minutes, until the tomatoes have reduced to a thick paste.

5 Taste the curry, and then add salt and pepper as seasoning, if it is needed. The curry should taste spicy, but not so hot that it burns your mouth.

6 Add the chopped fresh coriander to the curry, along with the garam masala. Garnish with fresh coriander leaves, and serve with slices of lime.

EATING IN INDIA   19

Chinese Homes in Harmony

In Chinese cities, all buildings were designed to be in harmony with each other and with nature. The direction they faced, their layout, and their proportions were all matters of great spiritual importance. Even the number of steps leading up to the entrance of the house was considered to be significant. House design in imperial China, before it became a republic in 1912, varied over time and between regions. In the hot and rainy south, courtyards tended to be covered for shade and shelter. In the drier north, courtyards were mostly open to the elements. Poor people in the countryside lived in simple, thatched huts. These were made from timber frames covered in mud plaster. They were often noisy, drafty, and overcrowded. In contrast, wealthy people had large, peaceful, and well-constructed homes. Many had beautiful gardens, filled with peonies, bamboo, and wisteria. Some gardens also contained orchards, ponds, and pavilions.

reception

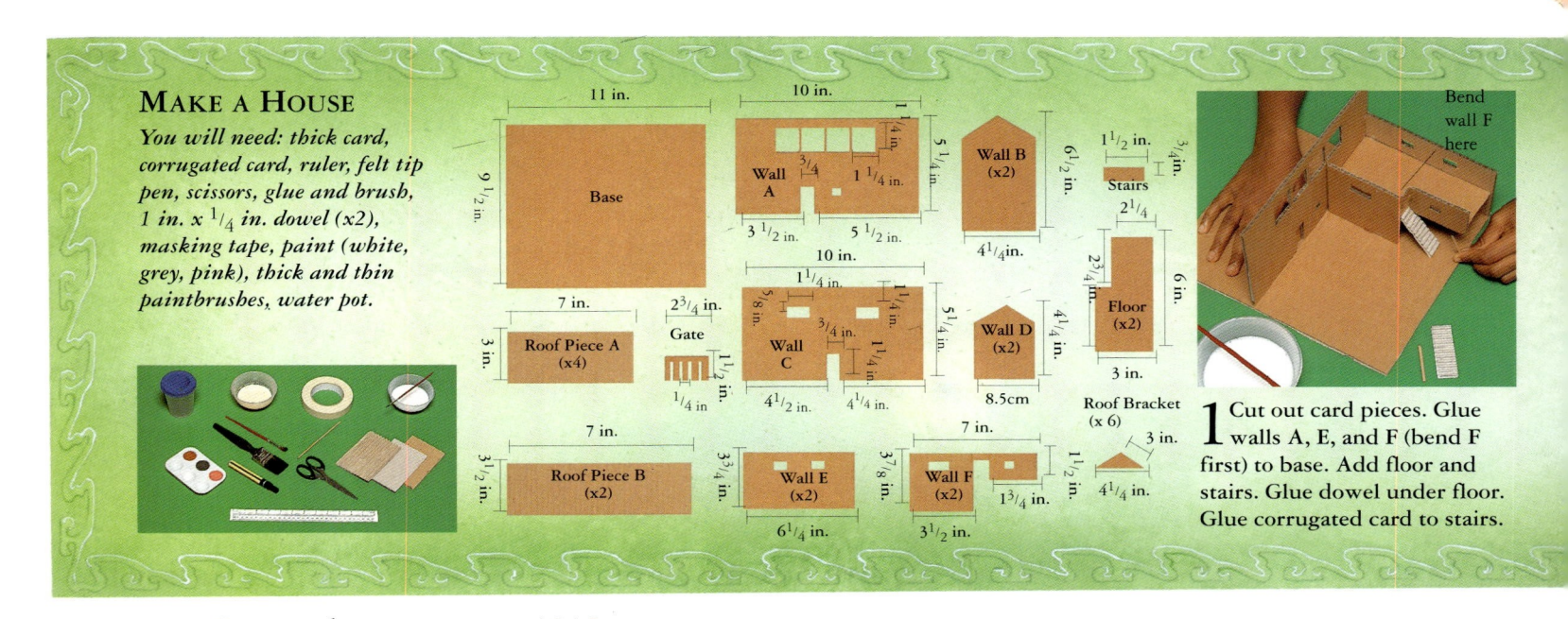

living quarters for owner's immediate family

watchtower

Inside a Han House
A wealthy family go about their daily lives in a Han dynasty (206 B.C.–A.D. 220) home. The house is built around several courtyards, with a garden at the side and a gatehouse leading into the streets. A watchtower gives a view of the world outside. The main family building at the rear is two stories high, but some homes had three or more floors.

main courtyard

Make a House
You will need: thick card, corrugated card, ruler, felt tip pen, scissors, glue and brush, 1 in. x 1/4 in. dowel (x2), masking tape, paint (white, grey, pink), thick and thin paintbrushes, water pot.

1 Cut out card pieces. Glue walls A, E, and F (bend F first) to base. Add floor and stairs. Glue dowel under floor. Glue corrugated card to stairs.

20 China 6000 B.C.–A.D. 1912

pond
garden
bridge
living quarters for other family members
round window
inner wall
horse and carriage
porch
gatehouse
outer wall
outer courtyard

Roof Charms
Decorative dragons and animals guard the roof of the Lama Temple in Beijing. Many Chinese homes also featured exotic figures such as these. People believed that they would ward off evil spirits.

The design of this model is based on houses built in southern China. The overhanging roofs cover the courtyard. This helps to keep out rain, and provides shelter from the sun.

2 To assemble second side, repeat method described in step 1. If necessary, hold pieces together with masking tape while the glue dries.

3 Glue B walls to the sides of the base, C wall to the back and D walls to the front. Hold with tape while glue dries. Glue gate between D walls.

4 Assemble A roofs (x2) and B roof (x1). Fix brackets underneath. Glue corrugated card (cut to same size as roof pieces), to top side of roofs.

5 Fix a small piece of card over the gate to make a porch. Paint house, as shown. Use a thin brush to create a tile effect on the removable roofs.

CHINESE HOMES IN HARMONY   21

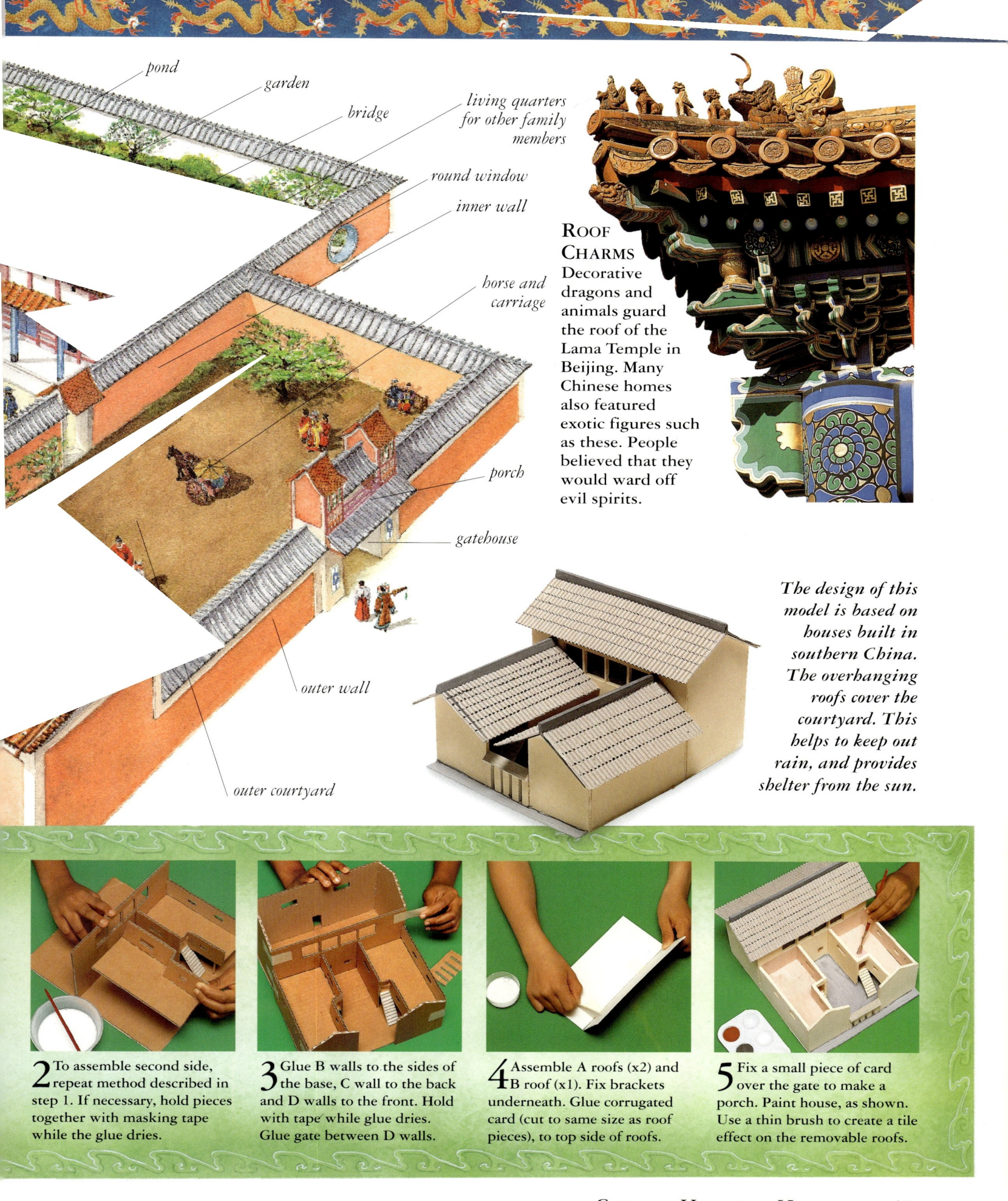

Traditional Life in China

THE THINKER, CONFUCIUS (Kong Fuzi) lived from 551 B.C. to 479 B.C. He taught that just as the emperor was head of the state, the oldest man was head of the household and should be obeyed by his family. In reality, his wife often controlled the lives of everyone in the household.

During the Han dynasty (206 B.C.–A.D. 220), noblewomen were kept apart from the outside world. They could only gaze at the streets from the watchtowers of their homes. It was not until the Song dynasty (A.D. 960–1279) that they had more freedom. In poor households, women worked all day, spending long, tiring hours farming, cooking, sweeping, and washing.

For children of poor families, education meant learning to do the work their parents did. This involved carrying goods to market, and helping with the threshing and planting. Wealthier children had private tutors at home. Boys who hope to become scholars or civil servants learned to read and write Chinese characters. They also studied math and the works of Confucius.

LESSONS FOR THE BOYS
This group of Chinese boys have their school lessons. In imperial China, boys usually received a more academic education than girls. Girls were mainly taught music, handicrafts, painting, and social skills. Some girls were taught academic subjects, but they were not allowed to take the civil service tests.

CHINESE MARRIAGE
A wedding ceremony takes place in the late 1800s. In imperial China, weddings were arranged by the parents of the bride and groom, rather than by the couples themselves. It was expected that the couple would respect their parents' wishes, even if they didn't like each other!

FOOT BINDING
This foot looks elegant in its beautiful slipper, but it's a different story when the slipper is removed. Just when life was improving for Chinese women, the cruel new custom of footbinding was introduced. Dancers had bound their feet for some years in the belief that it made them look dainty. In the Song dynasty, the custom spread to wealthy and noble families. Little girls of five or so had their feet bound up so tightly that they became terribly deformed.

TAKING IT EASY
A noblewoman living from the Qing dynasty relaxes on a garden terrace with her children (c.1840). She is very fortunate, since she has little else to do but enjoy the pleasant surroundings of her home. In rich families like hers, servants did most of the hard work, such as cooking, cleaning, and washing. Wealthy Chinese families kept many servants, who usually lived in quarters inside their employer's home. Servants accounted for a large number of the workforce in imperial China. During the Ming dynasty (1368–1644), some 9,000 maidservants were employed at the imperial palace in Beijing alone!

RESPECT AND HONOUR
Children in the 1100s bow respectfully to their parents. Confucius taught that people should value and honor their families, including their ancestors. He believed that this helped to create a more orderly and virtuous society.

THE EMPEROR AND HIS MANY WIVES
Sui dynasty emperor Yangdi (A.D. 581–618) rides with his many womenfolk. Like many emperors, Yangdi was surrounded by women. An emperor married one woman, who would then become his empress, but he would still enjoy the company of concubines (secondary wives).

TRADITIONAL LIFE IN CHINA   23

Food and Diet in China

Today, Chinese food is among the most popular in the world. Rice was the basis of most meals in ancient China, especially in the south, where it was grown. Northerners used wheat flour to make noodles and buns. Food varied greatly between the regions. The north was famous for pancakes, dumplings, lamb, and duck dishes. In the west, Sichuan was renowned for its hot chilli peppers. Mushrooms and bamboo shoots were popular along the lower Chang Jiang (Yangzi River).

For many people, meat was a rare treat. It included chicken, pork, and many kinds of fish, and was often spiced with garlic and ginger. Dishes featured meat that people from other parts of the world might find strange, such as turtle, dog, monkey and bear. Food was stewed, steamed, and fried. The use of chopsticks and bowls dates back to the Shang dynasty (*c.*1600–1122 B.C.).

THE KITCHEN GOD
A paper picture of the kitchen god and his wife hung in every kitchen. Each year, on the 24th day of the 12th month, sweets were put out as offerings. Then the picture was taken down and burned. A new one was hung in its place on New Year's Day.

A TANG BANQUET
In this picture, elegant ladies of the Tang court are sitting down to a feast. They are accompanied by music and singing, but there are no men present—women and men usually ate separately. This painting dates from the A.D. 900s, when raised tables came into fashion in China. Guests at banquets would wear their finest clothes. The most honored guest would sit to the east of the host, who sat facing south. The greatest honor of all was to be invited to dine with the emperor.

MAKE RED BEAN SOUP

You will need: measuring jug, food scale, measuring spoon, ½ lb. aduki beans, 3 tsp. ground nuts, 4 tsp. short-grain rice, cold water, tangerine, saucepan and lid, wooden spoon, ½ cup sugar, liquidizer, sieve, bowls.

1 Use the scale to weigh the aduki beans. Add the ground nuts and the short-grain rice. Measure 4 cups of cold water in the jug.

2 Wash and drain the beans and rice. Put them in a bowl. Add the cold water. Leave overnight to soak. Do not drain the water.

3 Wash and dry the tangerine. Then carefully remove the peel in a continuous strip. Leave the peel overnight, until it is hard and dry.

24   CHINA 6000 B.C.–A.D. 1912

THAT SPECIAL TASTE

The Chinese flavor their food with a variety of herbs and spices. Garlic has been used in Chinese dishes and sauces for thousands of years. It may be chopped, crushed, pickled, or served whole. Root ginger is another crucial Chinese taste. Fresh chili peppers are used to make fiery dishes, and sesame provides flavoring in the form of paste, oil, and seeds.

sesame

root ginger

SHANG BRONZEWARE FIT FOR A FEAST

This three-legged bronze cooking pot dates from the Shang dynasty (c.1600 B.C.–1122 B.C.). Its green appearance is caused by the reaction of the metal to air over the 3,500 years since it was made. During Shang rule, metalworkers made many vessels out of bronze, including cooking pots and wine jars. They were used in all kinds of ceremonies, and at feasts people held in honor of their dead ancestors.

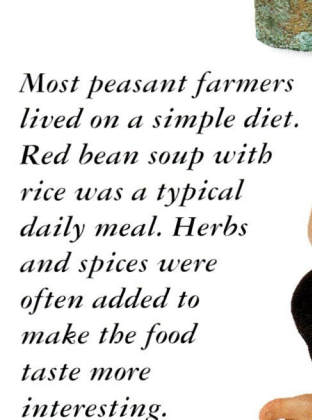

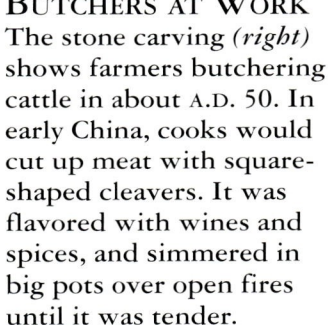

BUTCHERS AT WORK

The stone carving (right) shows farmers butchering cattle in about A.D. 50. In early China, cooks would cut up meat with square-shaped cleavers. It was flavored with wines and spices, and simmered in big pots over open fires until it was tender.

Most peasant farmers lived on a simple diet. Red bean soup with rice was a typical daily meal. Herbs and spices were often added to make the food taste more interesting.

4 Put the soaked beans and rice (plus the soaking liquid) into a large saucepan. Add the dried tangerine peel and 2 cups of cold water.

5 Bring the mixture to boiling point. Reduce the heat, cover the saucepan, and simmer for 2 hours. Stir occasionally. If the liquid boils away, add more water.

6 When the beans are just covered with the water, add the sugar. Simmer this until the sugar has completely dissolved.

7 Remove and discard the tangerine peel. Leave soup to cool, uncovered. Puree the soup. Strain any lumps with a sieve. Pour into bowls.

FOOD AND DIET IN CHINA 25

Family Life in Japan

FAMILIES IN EARLY JAPAN survived by working together in the family business or on the family land. Japanese people believed that the family group was more important than any one individual. Family members were supposed to consider the wellbeing of the whole family first, before thinking about their own needs and plans. Sometimes, this led to quarrels or disappointments. For example, younger brothers in poor families were often not allowed to marry, so that the family land could be handed on, undivided, to the eldest son. Daughters would leave home to marry if a suitable husband could be found. If not, they also remained single and stayed in their parents' house.

Family responsibility passed down the generations, from father to eldest son. Japanese families respected age and experience, because they believed it brought wisdom.

BRINGING UP BABY
It was women's work to care for young children. This painting shows an elegant young mother from a rich family dressing her son in a kimono (a robe with wide sleeves). The family maid holds the belt for the boy's kimono, and a pet cat watches nearby.

WORK
A little boy uses a simple machine to help winnow rice. (Winnowing separates the edible grains of rice from the outer husks.) Boys and girls from farming families were expected to help with work around the house and farmyard, and in the fields.

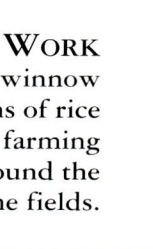

CARP STREAMER
You will need: pencil, 2 large sheets of paper, felt-tip pen, scissors, paints, paintbrush, water pot, glue, wire, masking tape, string, piece of cane.

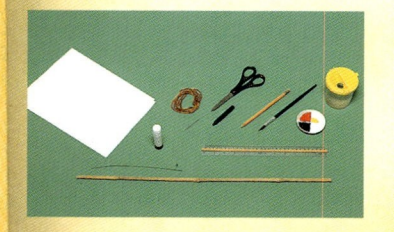

1 Take the pencil and one piece of paper. Draw a large carp fish shape on the paper. When you are happy with the shape, go over it in felt-tip pen.

2 Put the second piece of paper over the first. Draw around the fish shape. Next, draw a border around the second fish, and add tabs, as shown.

3 Add scales, eyes, fins, and other details to both of the fishes, as shown above. Cut them both out, remembering to snip into the tabs. Paint both fishes.

PLAYTIME
These young boys have started two tops spinning close to each other. They are waiting to see what will happen when the tops touch. Japanese children had many different toys with which to play. In addition to the spinning top, another big favorite was the kite.

TRADITIONAL MEDICINE
Kuzu (Japanese arrowroot) and ginger are ingredients that have been used for centuries as treatments in traditional Japanese medicine. Most traditional drugs are made from vegetables. The kuzu and ginger are mixed together in different ways, depending on the symptoms of the patient. For example, there are 20 different mixtures for treating colds. Ginger is usually used when there is no fever.

kuzu   *ginger*

HONORING ANCESTORS
A mother, father, and child make offerings and say their prayers at a small family altar in their house. The lighted candle and paper lantern help guide the spirits to their home. Families honored their dead ancestors at special festivals. At the festival of Obon, in the summer, they greeted family spirits who had returned to earth.

4 Put the two fish shapes together, with the painted sides out. Turn the tabs in and glue the edges of the fish together, except for the tail and the mouth.

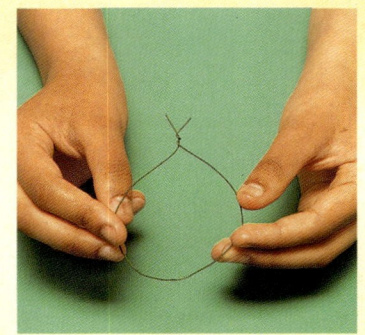

5 Use garden wire to make a ring the size of the mouth. Twist the ends together, then bend them back. Wrap masking tape around the ends.

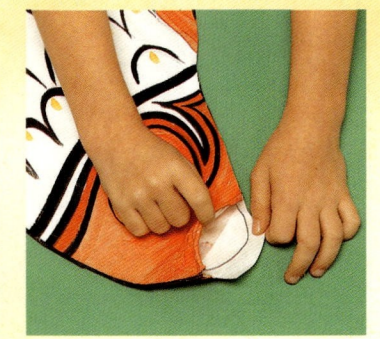

6 Place the ring in the fish's mouth. Glue the ends of the mouth over the ring. Tie one end of some string on to the mouth ring, and the other end to a garden cane.

Families fly carp streamers on Boy's Day (the fifth day of the fifth month) every year. One carp is flown for each son. Carp are symbols of perseverance and strength.

FAMILY LIFE IN JAPAN 27

Growing Up in Greece

CHILDREN IN EARLY TIMES faced many obstacles as they grew up. In ancient Greece, when a baby was born, its father would decide whether to keep or abandon it. A sick or handicapped baby might be left outdoors at birth. Whoever rescued the child could raise it as their slave. Girls were more likely to be rejected because they could not provide for their parents in adulthood. Many children died in infancy due to poor healthcare.

Education was considered to be important for boys. Even so, it was usually only sons in rich families who received a complete schooling. They were taught a variety of subjects, including reading, music and gymnastics. Boys from poor families often learned their father's trade. Education in domestic skills was essential for most girls. A notable exception was in Sparta, where the girls joined boys in hard physical training.

BABY STEPS
This baby is waving a rattle as he sits in a high chair. The chair also served as a potty. It might have wheels on it, to help the baby learn how to walk.

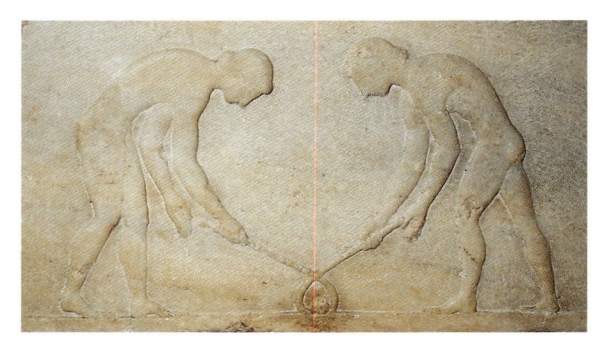

BULLY OFF
These two boys are playing a game similar to hockey. In general, team sports were ignored in favor of sports activities where an individual could excel. Wrestling and athletics are two such examples. They were encouraged as training for war.

YOU ARE IT
Two girls play a kind of tag game, in which the loser has to carry the winner. Girls had less free time than boys did. They were supposed to stay close to home and help their mothers with housework, cooking, and taking care of the younger children.

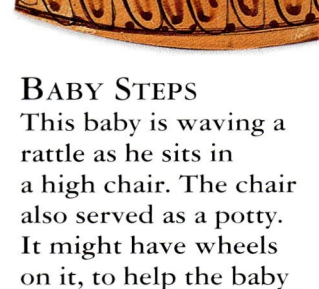

MAKE A SCROLL
You will need: 2 x 1 ft. rods of balsa wood, 2 in. in diameter, 4 doorknobs, double-sided sticky tape, sheet of paper 1 x 1 ft., 1 x 2 3/4 in. rod of balsa wood, 3/4 in. in diameter, craft knife, paintbrush, white glue, ink powder.

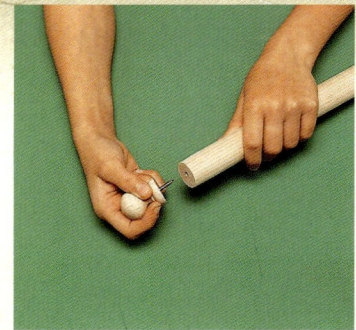

1 Carefully screw a door knob into both ends of each 1-foot rod of balsa wood, or ask an adult to do it for you. These are the end pieces of the scroll.

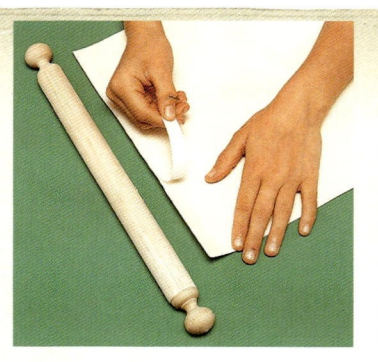

2 Cut two pieces of double-sided tape 12 inches long. Stick one piece of tape along the top of the paper and another along the bottom.

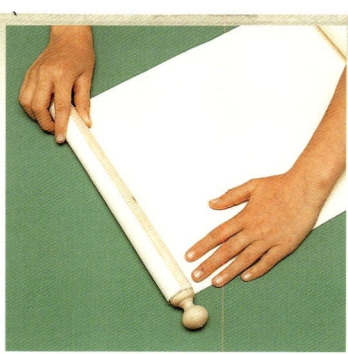

3 Wrap the top of the paper once around one of the pieces of balsa wood. Repeat this step again for the second piece at the bottom of the paper.

ACTION DOLL
The arms and legs on this terra-cotta figure are attached with cord, so that the shoulders and knees can be moved. A doll such as this was a luxury item, which only a wealthy family could afford to buy for its children. Other popular toys were rattles and hoops.

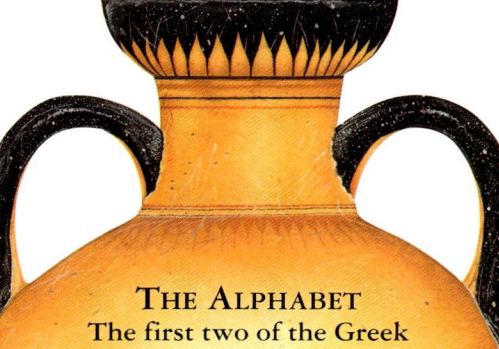

THE ALPHABET
The first two of the Greek alphabet's 24 letters are called alpha and beta—these names give us the English word "alphabet."

A	B	Γ	Δ	E	Z	H	Θ	I
A	B	G	D	E	Z	e	TH	I

K	Λ	M	N	Ξ	O	Π	P	Σ
K	L	M	N	X	O	P	R	S

T	Y	Φ	X	Ψ	Ω
T	U	PH	KH	PS	o

LIGHT OF LEARNING
This lamp takes the form of a teacher holding a scroll. Education involved learning poems and famous speeches from scrolls by heart. This was thought to help boys make effective speeches in court and at public meetings. Good orators were always admired, and could wield much influence.

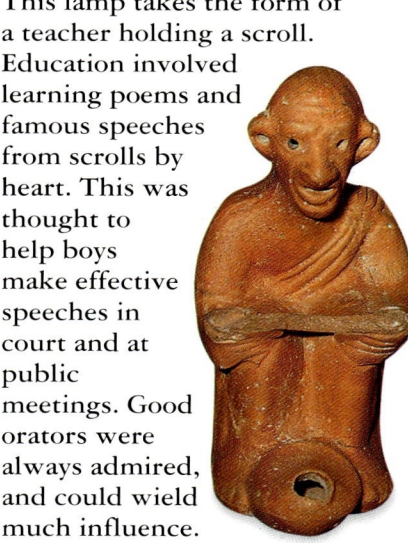

Scrolls in ancient Greece were usually made from animal skin.

A SECOND MOTHER
Greeks often hired wet nurses (*on the left*) to breastfeed their babies. Some nurses were forbidden to drink wine, in case it affected their milk, or made them so drunk that they might harm the baby.

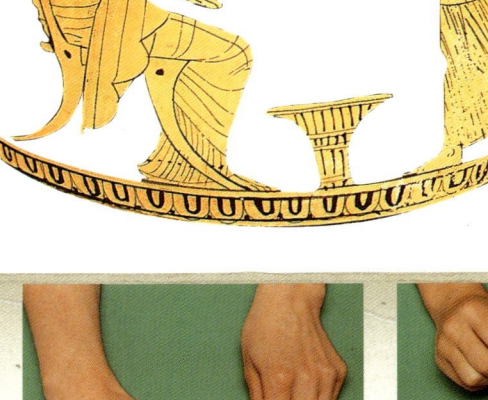

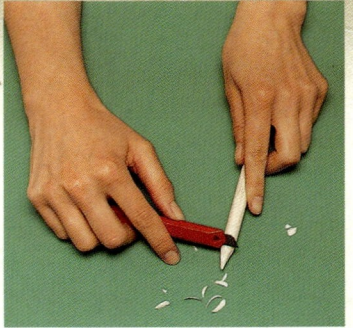

4 Ask an adult to help you with this step. Take the 2 ³⁄₄ piece of balsa wood, and use your craft knife to sharpen the end of it into a point.

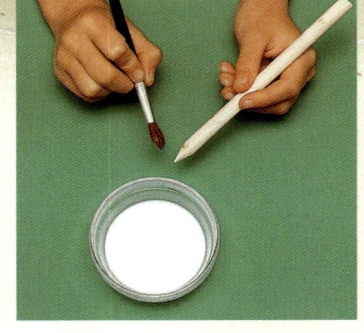

5 Paint the tip of your pen with glue. This will stop the wood from soaking up the ink. Add water to the ink powder to make ink.

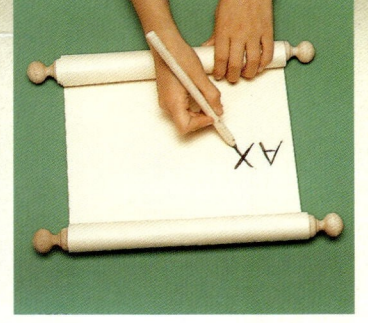

6 Write some letters or a word on your scroll with your pen. We've translated the Greek alphabet above in the fact box. Use this as a guide.

7 We have copied some letters in ancient Greek. You could also write a word. Ask a friend to translate what you have written using the alphabet.

GROWING UP IN GREECE 29

Roman Houses

During the Roman Era, wealthy citizens could afford to live in their own private house. A typical town house was designed to look inward, with the rooms arranged around a central courtyard and a walled garden. Outside walls had few windows, and these were small and shuttered. The front door opened onto a short passage that led into an airy courtyard called an atrium. Front rooms on either side of the passage were usually used as bedrooms. Sometimes they were used as workshops or shops, and they had shutters that opened to the street. The middle of the atrium was open to the sky. Below this opening was a pool, set into the floor, to collect rainwater. Around the atrium were more bedrooms and the kitchen. If you were a guest or had important business, you would be shown into the tablinium. The dining room, or triclinium, was often the grandest room of all. Very rich people also had a summer dining room overlooking the garden. Houses were made of local building materials. These might include stone, mud bricks, cement, and timber. Roofs were made of clay tiles.

garden

bedroom

tablinium (living room and office)

Locks and Keys
This was the key to the door of a Roman house. Pushed in through a keyhole, the prongs at the end of the key fitted into holes in the bolt in the lock. The key could then be used to slide the bolt along and unlock the door.

Inside a Roman Home
The outside of a wealthy Roman's town house was usually very plain, but inside it was highly decorated with elaborate wall paintings and intricate mosaics. The rooms were sparsely furnished, with couches and beds, small side tables, benches, and folding stools. There were few windows, but high ceilings and wide doors made the most of the light from the open atrium and the garden.

Make a Roman Home
You will need: pencil, ruler, thick card, scissors, white glue, paintbrushes, masking tape, corrugated cardboard, thin card, water pot, acrylic paints.

Cut out pieces of card according to the measurements shown.

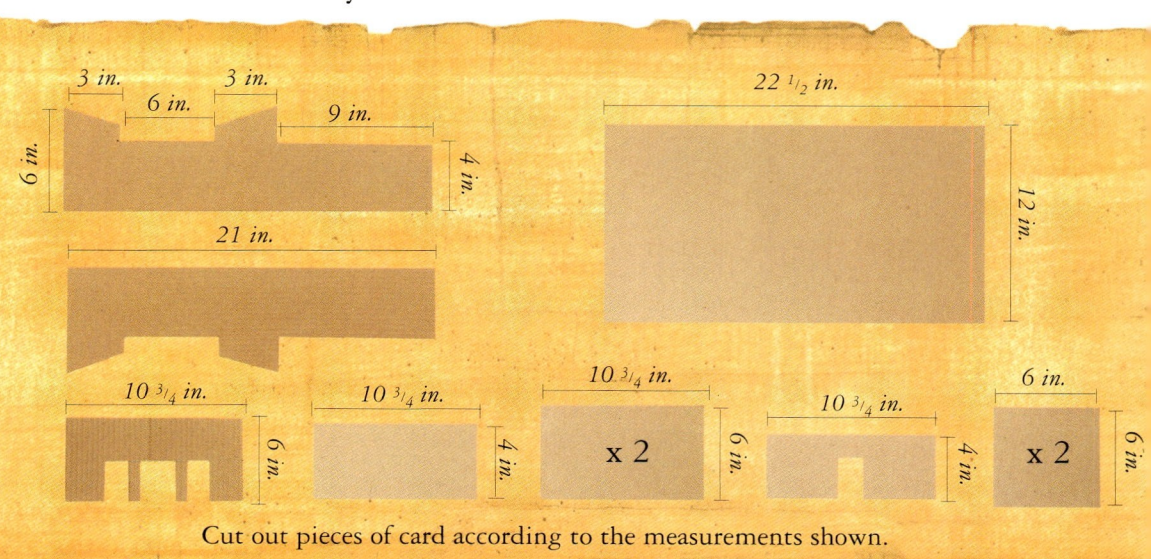

30 ROMAN EMPIRE 750 b.c.–a.d. 450

water spout

atrium (courtyard)

bedroom

GARDEN DELIGHTS
At the back of many Roman houses lay beautiful, walled gardens with stone columns, pools, fountains, statues, and terraces. People would eat out here on warm evenings, reclining on couches and surrounded by trailing ivy, sweet-smelling roses, irises, lilies, bay trees, and cypresses.

ivy

roses

triclinium (dining room)

kitchen

This Roman house has high, windowless walls to shut out the hot summer sun, which makes it cool and shady inside.

1 Cut out the pieces of thick card. Edge each piece with glue. Press the pieces together, and reinforce with masking tape. You have now made the walls of your house.

2 Measure your model and cut out pieces of corrugated cardboard for the roofs. Stick them together with glue, as shown above. Paint the roofs red.

3 Rainwater running down the sloped atrium roof was directed into a pool below by gutters and water spouts. Make gutters from strips of thin card, with holes as spouts.

4 Paint the house walls as shown, using masking tape to get a straight line. Glue on the roofs. Why not finish off your Roman house with some authentic graffiti!

ROMAN HOUSES 31

Family Occasions in Rome

THE FAMILY was very important to Romans. The father was the all-powerful head of the family, which included everyone in the household—the wife, children, slaves, and even close relatives. In the early days of Rome, a father had the power of life and death over his children! However, Roman fathers were rarely harsh, and children were much loved by both parents.

Childhood was fairly short. Parents would arrange for a girl to be betrothed at the age of 12, and a boy at 14. Marriages took place a few years later. Brides usually wore a white dress and a yellow cloak, with an orange veil and a wreath of sweetly scented flowers. A sacrifice would be made to the gods, and everyone would wish the couple well. That evening, a procession with flaming torches and flute music would lead the newly weds to their home.

Funerals were also marked with music and processions. By Roman law, burials and cremations had to take place outside the city walls.

Happy Families
This Roman tombstone from Germany shows a family gathered together for a meal. From the Latin inscription on it, we know that it was put up by a soldier of the legions, in memory of his dead wife. He lovingly describes her as the "sweetest and purest" of women.

Mother and Baby
A mother tends to her baby in the cradle. When children were born, they were laid at the feet of their father. If he accepted the child, he would pick it up. In wealthy families, a birth was a great joy, but for poorer families it just meant another mouth to feed. Romans named a girl on the eighth day after the birth, and a boy on the ninth day. The child was given a bulla, a charm to ward off evil spirits.

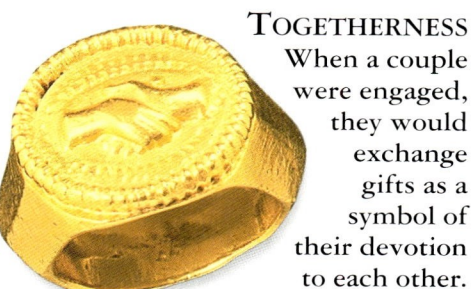

Togetherness
When a couple were engaged, they would exchange gifts as a symbol of their devotion to each other. A ring like this one might have been given by a man to his future bride. The clasped hands symbolize marriage. Gold pendants with similar patterns were also popular.

MOURNING THE DEAD

A wealthy Roman has died and his family have gone into mourning. Laments are played on flutes as they prepare his body for the funeral procession. The Romans believed that the dead went to Hades, the Underworld, which lay beyond the river of the dead. A coin was placed in the corpse's mouth, to pay the ferryman. Food and drinks for the journey were buried with the body.

TILL DEATH US DO PART

A Roman marriage ceremony was much like a present-day Christian wedding. The couple would exchange vows and clasp hands to symbolize their union. Here, the groom is holding the marriage contract, which would have been drawn up before the ceremony. Not everyone found happiness, however, and divorce was very common.

WEDDING FLOWERS

Roman brides wore a veil on their wedding day. This was often crowned with a wreath of flowers. In the early days of the Empire, verbena and sweet marjoram were a popular combination. Later fashions included orange blossom and myrtle, whose fragrant flowers were sacred to Venus, the goddess of love.

orange blossom

verbena

FAMILY OCCASIONS IN ROME

Roman Education

Most children in the Roman Empire never went to school. They either learned a trade from their parents, or studied math by trading on a market stall. Boys might be trained to fight with swords and to ride horses, in preparation for joining the army. Girls would be taught how to run the home, in preparation for marriage.

Wealthy families did provide an education for their sons, and sometimes for their daughters, too. They were usually taught at home by a private tutor, but there were also small schools. Tutors and teachers would teach children arithmetic, and how to read and write both Latin and Greek. Intelligent pupils might also learn public speaking skills, poetry, and history. Girls often had music lessons at home, on a harp-like instrument called a lyre.

INKPOTS AND PENS
A pen and ink were used to write on scrolls made from papyrus (a kind of reed) or thin sheets of wood. Ink was often made from soot or lamp-black, mixed with water. It was kept in inkpots such as these. Inkpots were made from glass, pottery, and metal. Pens were made from bone, reeds, and bronze.

WRITING IN WAX
This painting shows a couple from Pompeii. The man holds a parchment scroll. His wife is probably going through their household accounts. She holds a wax-covered writing tablet and a stylus, to scratch words into the wax. A stylus had a pointed end for writing and a flat end for erasing.

A WRITING TABLET

You will need: sheets and sticks of balsa wood, craft knife, ruler, white glue, paintbrush, brown acrylic paint, water pot, modeling clay, work board, rolling pin, modeling tool, skewer, purple thread, pencil (to be used as a stylus), gold paint.

1. Use the craft knife to cut the balsa sheet into two rectangles, 4 x 8 3/4 in. The sticks of balsa should be cut into four pieces 8 3/4 in. long, and four pieces 4 in. long.

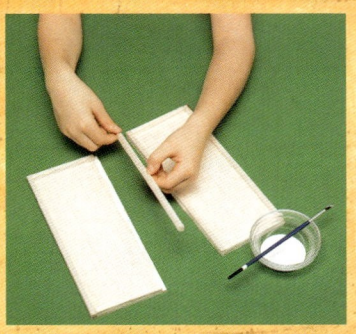

2. Glue the sticks around the edges of each sheet as shown. These form a shallow hollow into which you can press the "wax." Paint the two frames a rich brown color.

3. Roll the modeling clay on a board, and place a balsa frame on top. Use the modeling tool to cut around the outside of the frame. Repeat this step.

34 ROMAN EMPIRE 750 B.C.–A.D. 450

TEACHER AND PUPILS
A stone sculpture from Roman Germany shows a teacher seated between two of his pupils. They are reading their lessons from papyrus scrolls. Children had to learn poetry and other writings by heart. Any bad behavior or mistakes were punished with a beating.

WRITING IT DOWN
Various materials were used for writing. Melted beeswax was poured into wooden trays to make writing tablets. Letters were scratched into the wax, which could be used again and again. Powdered soot was mixed with water to make ink for writing on papyrus, parchment, and wood.

melted beeswax

soot

Roman numerals on papyrus

I	II	III	IV	V
1	2	3	4	5
VI	VII	VIII	IX	X
6	7	8	9	10

LETTERS IN STONE
Temples, monuments, and public buildings were covered in Latin inscriptions, such as this one. Each letter was beautifully chiseled by a stonemason. These words are carved in marble. The inscription marked the 14th birthday of Lucius Caesar, the grandson of the Emperor Augustus.

4 Cut off about 1/2 in. all around the edge of each modeling clay rectangle. This helps to make sure that the modeling clay will fit inside the balsa wood frame.

5 Carefully press the clay into each side—this represents the wax. Use the skewer to poke two holes through the inside edge of each frame, as shown.

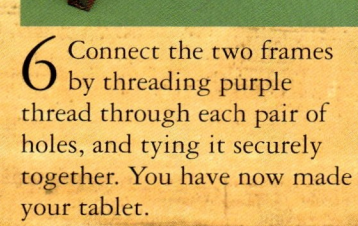

6 Connect the two frames by threading purple thread through each pair of holes, and tying it securely together. You have now made your tablet.

Paint the pencil gold to make it look like it is made from metal. Use it like a stylus to scratch words on your tablet. Why not try writing in Latin? You could write **CIVIS ROMANVS SVM,** *which means, "I am a Roman citizen."*

ROMAN EDUCATION 35

Life on a Celtic Farm

MEN, WOMEN, AND CHILDREN were all expected to play their parts in running a Celtic farm. It seems likely that both men and women worked in the fields. Men usually did the ploughing, but the women probably performed tasks such as weeding the crops. Everyone helped at harvest time, because it was vital to gather the grain as soon as it was ripe. There were countless other jobs that needed doing to keep the farm running smoothly, such as combing sheep, caring for sick animals, milking cows, collecting eggs, repairing thatched roofs, and fetching water. Along with all the other tasks around the farm, parents had to teach their children the skills they would need in adult life. Many Celtic parents sent their sons and daughters to live in other households until they were grown up. This was a way of making close bonds of friendship between families and tribes, and italso taught the children extra skills.

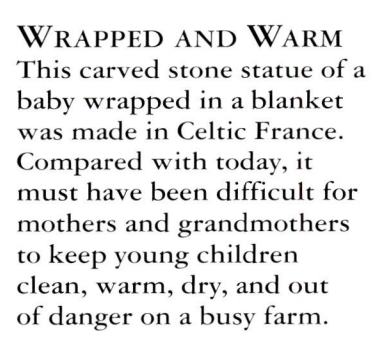

WRAPPED AND WARM
This carved stone statue of a baby wrapped in a blanket was made in Celtic France. Compared with today, it must have been difficult for mothers and grandmothers to keep young children clean, warm, dry, and out of danger on a busy farm.

LOCKED UP
Keys lie these were used to lock wooden chests full of valuable goods, such as the family's marriage wealth. This was the bride's dowry (money and treasure from her father), plus an equal amount given by the husband on their wedding day. In some Celtic lands, wives had the right to inherit this if they outlived their husbands.

MAKE A POT

You will need: paper, bowl, white glue, water, balloon, petroleum jelly, card, compass, pencil, ruler, scissors, masking tape, cardboard core from roll of tape, pin, red and black paint, paintbrushes.

1 To make papier-mâché, tear paper or newspaper into small strips. Fill a bowl with 1 part glue to 3 parts water. Add the paper pieces and soak.

2 Blow up the balloon and cover in petroleum jelly. Cover the balloon in a layer of papier-mâché mixture. Allow to dry, then slowly build up more layers.

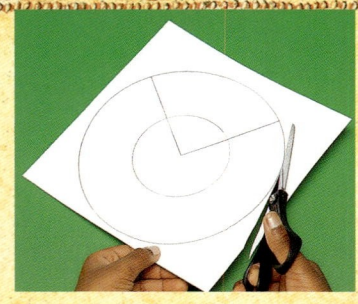

3 Draw a circle 8 in. in diameter on the card. Draw a second circle inside, 3¾ in. in diameter. Mark a quarter of both circles. Cut out the large circle.

36 THE CELTS 800 B.C.–A.D. 1066

DYED IN THE WOOL

The Romans reported that the Celts liked patterned, bright-colored clothes. Sheep's wool was often dyed before being woven into cloth. Dyes were made from flowers, bark, berries, leaves, and lichen boiled together with salt, crushed rock, and stale urine. The wool was soaked in this mixture then boiled again or left to soak for several hours.

sheep's wool   lichen

HAND-WOVEN

Many Celtic women made clothes and blankets from sheep's wool from their own farms. First, they cleaned and sorted the wool, then they spun it into thread. The thread was woven on an upright loom. Heavy weights kept the warp (vertical) threads straight while the weft (horizontal) thread was passed in between.

BUTTER BUCKET

Wooden buckets such as this were used on many Celtic farms, but few have survived. This one was found buried in a bog in northern Scotland. It contained butter. The damp, airless conditions in the bog had stopped the wood from rotting.

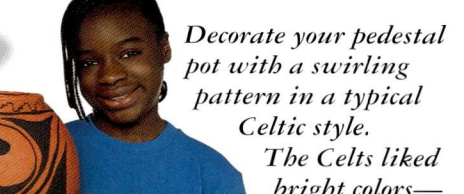

PEDESTAL POTS

Celtic women made simple pottery bowls and dishes for use at home. Wealthy Celtic people could also afford elegant vases and jugs like these pedestal pots (pots with feet), made by expert craftspeople in towns.

Decorate your pedestal pot with a swirling pattern in a typical Celtic style. The Celts liked bright colors— the pot that inspired this model was originally bright red.

4 Cut out a quarter of the outer circle and all of the inner circle, as shown. The outer circle will be the pot base. Stick the ends together with tape.

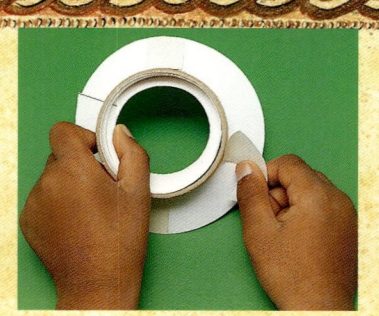

5 Use the cardboard inner circle from a roll of tape to make the stem of the pot. Attach it to the card base with masking tape.

6 Pop the balloon with a pin. Cut off the top end of the pot evenly. Attach the base and stem to the bottom of the pot with masking tape.

7 Paint the whole pot with red paint, including the stem and neck. Then add the Celtic pattern, as shown above, with black paint.

LIFE ON A CELTIC FARM   37

Celtic Food and Drink

Food was very important to the Celts. They enjoyed eating and drinking, and were not ashamed of getting drunk, or of rowdy behavior. They did not, however, approve of people getting too fat. Roman writers reported that Celtic warriors were ordered not to let out their belts, but to lose weight, when clothes around their waists became too tight! The Celts produced most of their own food on their farms. They needed to buy only items such as salt (used to preserve meat and fish), and luxury goods such as wine. They also hunted and fished for many wild creatures, and gathered wild fruits, nuts, herbs, and mushrooms from meadows and forests. Celtic families were famous throughout Europe for their hospitality to strangers. It was their custom to offer food and drinks to any visitor, and not to ask who they were or where they were from until the end of the meal.

Hanging Cauldron
Meals for large numbers of people were cooked in a big cauldron. This bronze cauldron, iron chain and hook were made around 300 B.C. in Switzerland. A cauldron could also be used for boiling water, heating milk to make cheese, and brewing mead.

Celtic Casserole
Meat, beans, grains, and herbs were stewed in a covered clay pot. The pot could be placed directly on glowing embers, or (as shown here) balanced on a hearthstone. This stone hearth, with a hollow pit for the fire, was found at an oppidum (Celtic town) in France.

Make some Oatcakes
You will need: 2 cups oatmeal, 2/3 cup flour, salt, baking soda, 1/2 stick butter, water, bowl, sifter, wooden spoon, small saucepan, heat-resistant glass, board, rolling pin, baking tray, wire rack.

1 Preheat the oven to 425°F. Put 2 cups of oatmeal into a large bowl. Add the flour and sift it into the bowl, with the oatmeal.

2 Next add 1 teaspoon of salt to the oatmeal and flour mix. Mix all the ingredients in the bowl together thoroughly, using a wooden spoon.

3 Add a quarter teaspoon of baking soda to the oatmeal and flour. Mix together thoroughly, and then put the bowl to one side.

38   THE CELTS 800 B.C.–A.D. 1066

GRINDING GRAIN
All kinds of grain were ground into flour using hand-powered querns (mills) like this one. The grains were poured through a hole in the top stone. This stone was turned around and around. The grains became trapped and were crushed between the top and bottom stones, then spilled out of the quern sides as flour.

FRUITS FROM THE FOREST
The Celts liked eating many of the same fruits and nuts that we enjoy today. However, they had to go and find them growing on bushes and trees. We know that the Celts ate fruit, because archaeologists have found many seeds and stones on garbage heaps and in lavatory pits at Celtic sites.

wild cherries
apples
blackberries
hazelnuts

OUT HUNTING
Celtic men hunted and fished for sport, and also as a way of finding food. This stone carving, which shows a huntsman and his dogs chasing deer, was made around A.D. 800 in Scotland. By then, Celtic power had declined, but many traditions persisted.

Enjoy your oatcakes plain, like the Celts did, or eat them with butter, cheese, or honey. All these were favorite Celtic foods. Today, some people put jam on their oatcakes, but sugar (used to make jam) was unknown in Europe in Celtic times.

4 Next, melt the butter in a small saucepan over low heat. Make sure that it does not burn. Add the melted butter to the oats and flour.

5 Boil some water. Put a little water in a mug or heat-resistant glass. Gradually add the boiled water to the mix, enough to make a stiff dough.

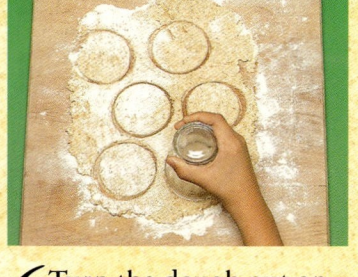

6 Turn the dough out on a board sprinkled with a little oatmeal and flour. Roll the dough until it is about $1/2$ in. thick. Cut the dough into 24 circles.

7 Put the circles of dough on a greased baking tray. Bake in the oven for 15 minutes. Allow the oatcakes to cool on a wire rack before serving.

CELTIC FOOD AND DRINK

Viking Family Life

In early times, everybody in the family knew who was related to whom, and where they lived. For the Vikings, even distant relatives played an important role in the family, in addition to grandparents, aunts, and uncles. They were all very aware of family links, and loyalty was fierce. If one member of a family was harmed, then the other members of the family would seek revenge. This led to feuds—quarrels between one family and another—that simmered from one generation to the next. Feuds could lead to fights, burglaries, and sometimes even murder.

The father of the household had great power over other members of the family. If he thought a newborn baby was a weakling, he could leave it to die. When a Viking farmer died, his eldest son inherited the farm. The rest of the family would have to move away, and the younger sons had to find new land of their own to farm. Mothers were often strong, determined women who had great influence in the family. There was little schooling. Learning how to fight with a sword or use an ax was more important than reading and writing. As children grew up, they were expected to work hard and to help around the house. They were sometimes fostered by families on other farms and had to work in return for their keep.

Helping Out
This reconstruction of a market stall in Jorvik shows a young boy helping his parents during a day's trading. Children often followed in the same trade as their parents. This boy would have learned how to haggle over prices. He would also know how to weigh silver.

Family Memorials
The Vikings often put up memorial stones to honor relatives and friends when they died. This stone from Sweden was put up by Tjagan and Gunnar in loving memory of their brother Vader.

Living in Fear
Old tales tell how Vikings fought each other mercilessly during long, bitter feuds between families. Murderous bands might turn up at a longhouse by night, threatening to burn down the roof and kill everybody inside. Viking households also risked attack from local peoples and other raiders wherever they settled.

Wanting Children
A woman who wanted to make a good marriage and have children would pray to Frey, the god of love and fertility. On these gold foil charms from Sweden, Frey is shown with his beautiful wife Gerda. She was the daughter of a giant called Gymir.

Growing Up
Children were expected to work hard in Viking times. Boys were taught farming, rowing, and sailing. Girls were taught how to spin and weave, milk cows, and prepare food. When all the daily tasks had been done, boys probably played games or went fishing. Viking girls may have spent some of their free time gathering berries and mushrooms.

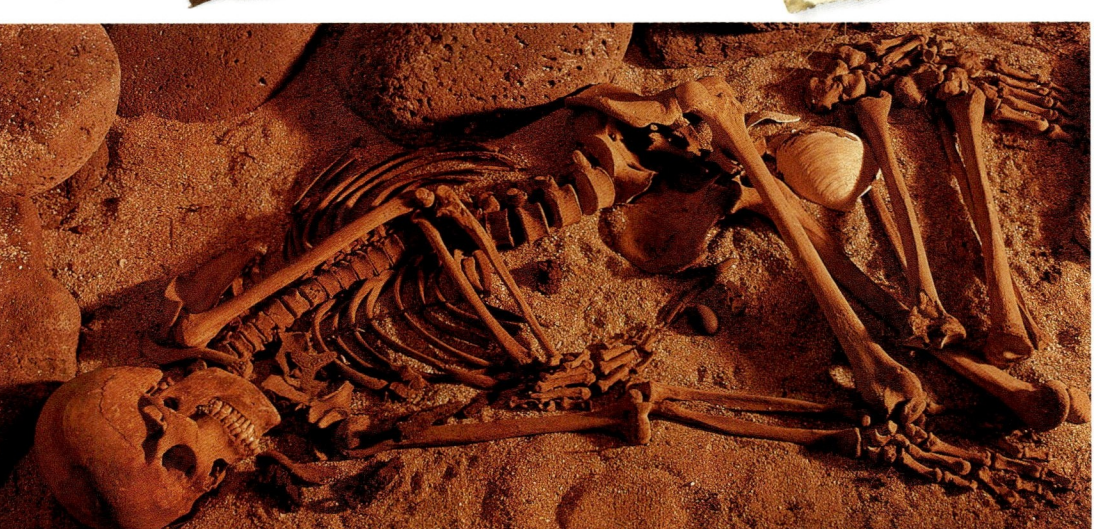

Burial Grave
This skeleton belongs to a Viking woman from Iceland. Archaeologists have been able to tell how women lived in the Viking age by examining the goods placed in their graves. These were possessions for them to use in the next world.

Viking Women

WOMEN WERE not allowed to speak in Viking public assemblies, where laws and judgements were passed, yet they had more independence than many European women at the time. They could choose their own husband, own property, and be granted a divorce. At a wedding, both the bride and groom had to make their marriage vows before witnesses. Memorial stones show that many husbands loved their wives and treated them with respect.

It was the women who usually managed the farm while their men were off raiding or trading. They never knew if their husbands, brothers, and sons would return from their travels or be lost in a storm at sea. Women certainly needed to be tough in the harsh landscapes and cold climates of countries such as Iceland and Greenland. It was their job to make woolen or linen clothes for the family, to prepare and cook food, and to clean the home.

WELCOME HOME
A woman in typical Viking dress welcomes a warrior returning from the wars. She has long hair tied back by a scarf, and is wearing a pleated dress. The woman is a valkyrie, one of Odin's maidens in Valholl. This charm comes from Öland in Sweden.

A DAY'S WORK
In this reconstruction from Jorvik (York, England), a Viking woman goes out to fetch water from the well. Hissing geese beat their wings and scatter in her path. Women's work lasted from dawn until nightfall, with clothes to darn, poultry to tend, meals to cook, and children to scold! Most women also spent several hours a day spinning and weaving wool into cloth to make clothes.

PRACTICAL BUT PRETTY
Viking women wore long tunics fastened by a pair of brooches. This Viking brooch was found in Denmark. It is over 1,000 years old, and is made of gold. Women wore clothing that was both practical and comfortable.

GETTING READY
Before a wedding or a visit to the fair, a Viking woman may have smoothed or pleated her dress on a board like this one. A glass ball would have been used instead of an iron. This whalebone board comes from Norway.

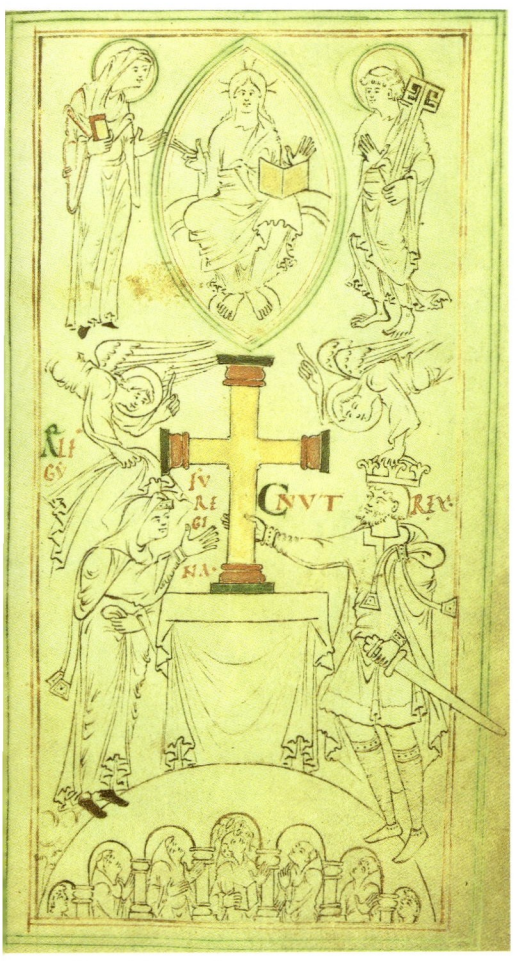

WEAVING AT HOME
Viking looms were much like this one. The warps, or upright threads, hang from a crossbar. The weft, or cross threads, pass between them to make cloth. Weaving was done by women in every Viking home.

THE NEW QUEEN
In this picture, Queen Aelfgyfu is shown alongside her husband King Cnut, in England. Aelfgyfu was Cnut's second wife. They are placing a cross on an altar. Queens were the most powerful women in Scandinavian society.

BELOVED WIFE
This stone was put up by King Gorm as a monument to his wife. The inscription reads "King Gorm made this memorial to his wife Thyri, adornment of Denmark." The messages written on such stones show the qualities that Vikings admired most in women.

North American Homes

Native American peoples built houses that were cleverly adapted to their surroundings. During the winter months, the Inuit of the far north built dome-shaped homes out of blocks of ice or with hard soil, wood, and whale bones. Where wood was plentiful, such as in the eastern part of the United States, people built a variety of homes. The wikiup, or wigwam, was dome shaped and made out of thatch, bark, or hide, which was tightly woven across an arch of bent branches. Basic, rectangular thatched houses were built from a construction of chopped twigs covered with a mix of clay and straw, or mud. Near the East Coast, massive longhouses, up to 150 feet long, with barrel-shaped roofs, were made from local trees. Some tribes lived in different kinds of shelters depending on the season. The Plains nations lived mostly in tipis (hide tents) and earth lodges. The nearest to modern buildings were the homes of the Pueblos in the Southwest. These were terraced, mud brick villages. Pueblos also built round underground ceremonial chambers with hidden entrances in the roof.

At Home
A Mandan chief relaxes with his family and dogs inside his lodge. Notice how a hole is cut in the roof, to let out smoke from the fire and let fresh air in. Earth lodges were popular with Mandan and Hidatsa people on the Upper Missouri. The layout followed strict customs. The family would sleep on the south side; guests slept on the north. Stores and weapons were stored at the back. The owner of this home has his horse inside, to prevent it from being stolen when the family is asleep.

Homes on the Plains
The hides of around 12 buffaloes were used to cover a family tipi that belonged to a Plains family. "Tipi" comes from a Siouan word meaning "to dwell." Hides were sewn together and stretched over wooden poles about 25 feet high. When it became too hot inside, the tipi sides were rolled up. In the winter, a fire was lit in the center.

Totem Pole
Totem poles were usually found in the northwestern corner of the United States. They were carved out of wood, often from the mighty red cedar (thuja) trees. Tall totem poles were erected outside the long plank houses of the Haida people. These homes were shared by several families. The poles were carved and painted to keep a record of the family histories of the people inside. They were also sometimes made to honor a great chief.

Earth Lodges
Mandan people perform the Buffalo Dance in front of their lodges. These were built with logs to create a dome frame, which was then covered over with tightly packed earth.

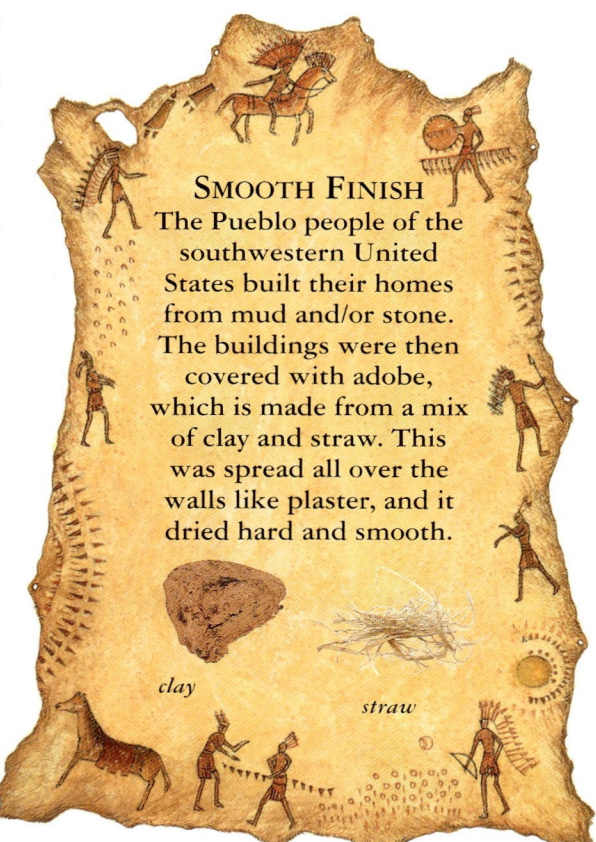

Layers of Brick
This ruin was once part of a complex of Pueblo buildings. Pueblo homes were often multistoried with flat roofs. The floors were reached by ladders. Circular brick chambers were built underground. These were the kivas used for religious and ceremonial rites.

Smooth Finish
The Pueblo people of the southwestern United States built their homes from mud and/or stone. The buildings were then covered with adobe, which is made from a mix of clay and straw. This was spread all over the walls like plaster, and it dried hard and smooth.

clay *straw*

The Longhouse
The Iroquois people of the Woodlands built long wooden houses. The frames were made of poles hewn from tree trunks, with cladding made from sheets of thick bark. Homes were communal. Many families lived in one longhouse, each with their own section built around an open fire.

holes in the roof let out smoke

sleeping platform

higher platform for storing food

groups of longhouses were built together, sometimes inside a protective fence.

Tribal Family Roles

Roles within the tribal North American family were well defined. The men were the hunters, protectors, and leaders. Women tended the crops, made clothes, cared for the home and the sick, and prepared the food. The children's early days were carefree, but they quickly learned to respect their elders. From an early age, young girls were taught the skills of craftwork and homemaking by their mothers, and the boys learned to use weapons and hunt from the men. Girls as young as 12 years old could be married. Boys had to exchange presents with their future in-laws before the marriage was allowed to take place. At birth, most children were named by a grandparent. Later, as adults, they could choose another name of their own.

HOLDING THE BABY
A woman holds her baby strapped to a cradleboard. Domestic scenes were often the focus of crafts, which reflected the importance of family life.

BONES FOR DINNER
This spoon was carved from animal bone. For the early family, there were no metal utensils. Many items were made from bone, tusks, antlers, and horns. Bone was also used to make bowls.

A DAY'S HUNTING
Blackfoot girls watch as men leave camp on a hunting trip. They are in search of bison. If the hunt is successful, the women will help skin the animals, then stretch out the hides to dry. Buffalo skins were used to make tipi covers. Softer buckskin, from deer, was used for clothing.

MAKE A KACHINA DOLL

You will need: cardboard roll, ruler, scissors, compass, pencil, thick card, white glue, brush for glue, masking tape, paints in cream/yellow, green/blue red and black, paintbrush, water pot, red paper.

1 Take the cardboard roll and cut a section of about a third off of the top. This will form the head piece. The larger end will form the body.

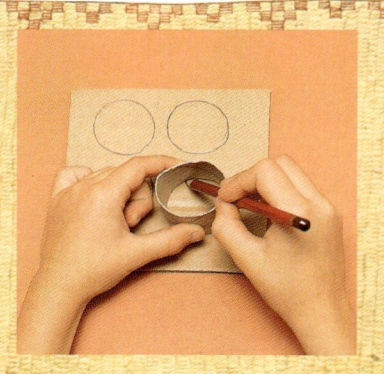

2 Use the compass (or end of the cardboard roll) to draw four circles about 1-in. radius on card. Then draw a smaller circle $3/4$ in. radius. Cut them all out.

3 Glue the larger circles to both ends of both of the cardboard roll tubes. Allow to dry. Glue the smaller circle of card on top of one end of the longer roll.

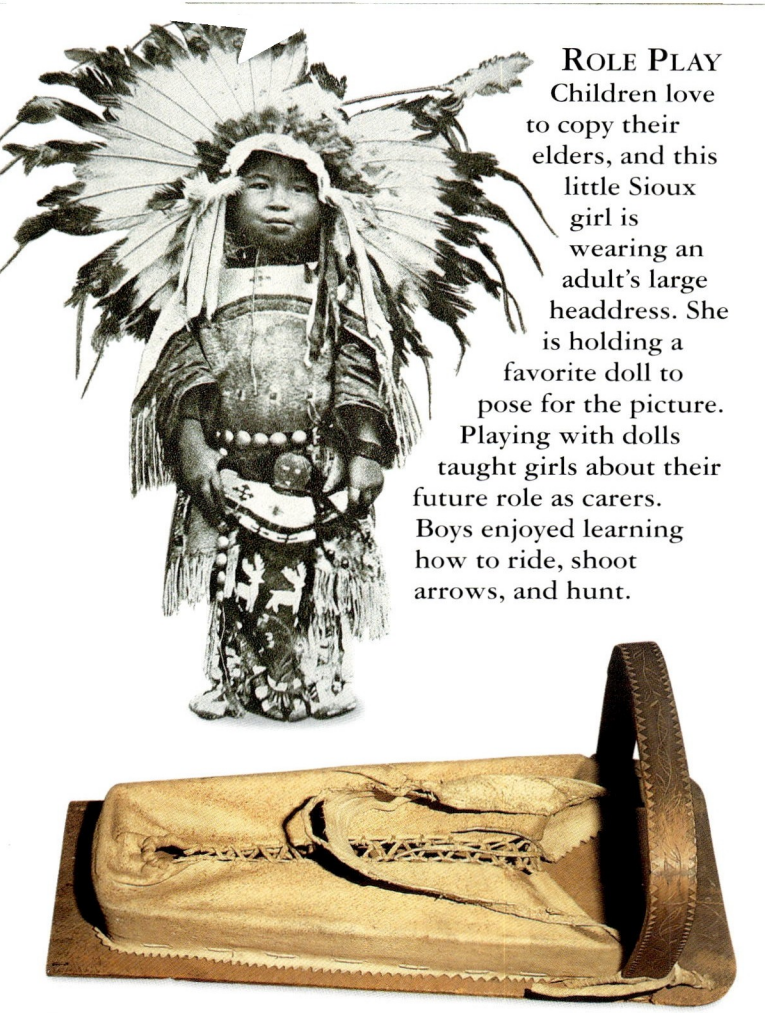

ROLE PLAY
Children love to copy their elders, and this little Sioux girl is wearing an adult's large headdress. She is holding a favorite doll to pose for the picture. Playing with dolls taught girls about their future role as carers. Boys enjoyed learning how to ride, shoot arrows, and hunt.

FAMILY GATHERING
A family from the Cree nation in Canada enjoys a quiet evening around the fire. Native American families were usually small, since no more than two or three children survived the harsh life. However, a lodge was often home to an extended family. There could be two or three sisters, their families, and grandparents under one roof.

BABY CARRIER
For the first year of its life, a baby would spend its time strapped to a cradleboard, such as this one inspired by the eastern Woodland tribes. It was also used by eastern Sioux, Iowa, Pawnee, and Osage parents. A baby could sleep or be carried in safety in its cradle, leaving the mother free to work. The board was strapped to the mother's back.

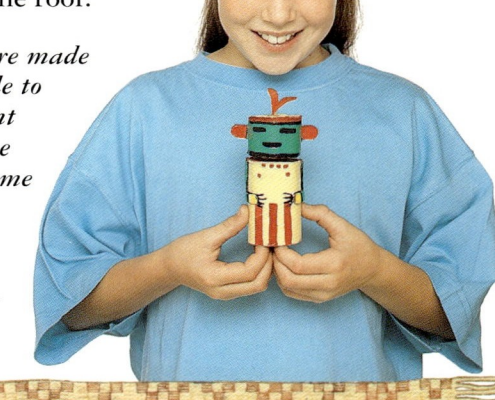

Kachina dolls were made by the Hopi people to represent different spirits. This is the Corn kachina. Some parents gave the dolls to their children to help them learn about tribal customs.

4 The smaller cardboard circle forms the doll's neck. Glue the small cardboard roll (the head) on top of the larger cardboard roll (the body).

5 Cut two small L-shapes from card to form the arms. Then cut two small ear shapes from the card. Cover these shapes with masking tape.

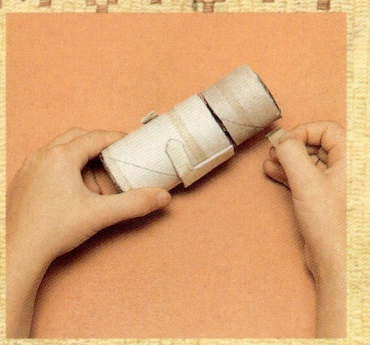

6 Glue the arms to the body, and the ears to the sides of the head, so that they stick out at right angles. Paint the doll the colors shown above.

7 While the paint is drying, cut two small feather shapes from red paper. Glue these to the top of the doll's head, so that they stick into the air.

TRIBAL FAMILY ROLES 47

Cold-Climate Homes

MOST ANCIENT ARCTIC GROUPS lived in small villages that contained a few families at most. The villages were spread out over a wide area, so each group had a large territory in which to hunt. In the winter, the Inuit, Saami, and other arctic tribes lived in sturdy houses that were built partly underground to protect them from the freezing conditions above. In the summer, or when they traveled from place to place, they lived in tents or temporary shelters.

In Siberia and parts of Scandinavia, groups such as the Nenets did not settle in one place. Their homes were lightweight tents—called chums in Siberia—which were frameworks made from wooden poles, covered with animal skins. Chums could withstand severe arctic blizzards, and kept

TENT LIFE
A Nenet herder loads a sled outside his family's chum in preparation for another day's travel across Siberia. Chums were convenient, light, and easy to assemble and dismantle. Some Nenets still live in chums, as their ancestors have done for many generations.

BUILDING MATERIALS
A deserted building made from stone and whale bone stands on a cliff in Siberia. Building materials were scarce in the Arctic. In coastal regions, people built houses with whale bones and driftwood gathered from the beach. Inland, houses were mainly built with rocks and turf.

ARCTIC DWELLING
This illustration shows a house in subarctic Alaska, with a section removed to show how it is made. Houses such as this one were buried under the ground. People entered by ladder through the roof.

MAKE A NENET TENT
You will need: 3 blankets (two 6½ x 5 ft. and one 4 x 4 ft.), tape measure, string, scissors, 10 bamboo sticks (nine 5 ft. long and one 1 ft. long), black marker pen, black thread, a log or a stone.

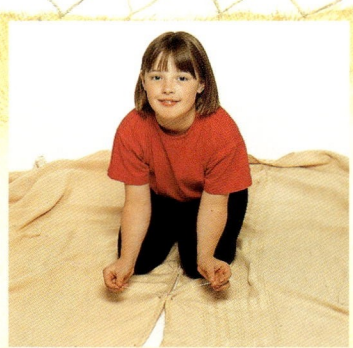

1. Cut small holes 4 in. apart along the shorter sides of the two large blankets. Thread a piece of string through the holes, and tie the string together.

2. Cut a 1 ft. 10 in. piece of string. Tie the 1-ft.-long stick and a black marker 22 in. apart. Use the marker to draw a circle on the smaller blanket.

3. Tie four bamboo sticks together at one end. Open out the sticks on the base blanket. Put the sticks on the edge of the circle so they stand up.

48 THE ARCTIC 10,000 B.C.–PRESENT

BONY BUNKER
Whale bone rafters arch over the remains of a home in Siberia. Part of the house was often built underground. First, the builders dug a pit to make the floor. Then they built low walls of rocks and turf. Long bones or driftwood laid on top of the walls formed sturdy rafters that supported a roof made from turf and stones.

MAKING WINDOWS
An old stone and turf house stands in arctic Greenland. Ancient peoples made windows by stretching a dried seal bladder over a hole in the wall. The bladder was thin enough to let light through.

A tent covered with several layers of animal skins made an extremely warm arctic home, even in the bitterly cold winter. The wooden poles were lashed together with rope.

4 Lean the five extra bamboo sticks against the main frame, placing the ends around the base circle. Leave a gap at the front for the entrance.

5 Tie the middle of the edge of the two larger blankets to the back of the frame, at the top. Make two tight knots to secure the blankets.

6 Bring each blanket around to the entrance. Tie them at the top with string. Roll the blankets down to the base, so that they lie flat on the frame.

7 Tie five 40 in. pieces of thread along the front edge of the blanket. Pull these tight, and tie to a log or stone to weigh down the base of the tent.

COLD-CLIMATE HOMES 49

Arctic Seasonal Camps

SUMMER IS A BUSY TIME for arctic animals and plants. The lives of arctic peoples changed with the seasons, too. The rising temperature melts the sea ice, and the oceans teem with tiny organisms called plankton. On land, the tundra explodes into flower. Insects hatch and burrowing creatures, such as lemmings, leave their tunnels in search of food. Wild reindeer, whales, and many types of birds migrate to the Arctic to feast on the plentiful supply of food.

In Canada, Alaska, and Greenland, the Inuit left their winter villages and traveled to the summer hunting grounds. They hunted fish and sea mammals, and gathered fruits and berries, taking advantage of the long, bright summer days.

During winter hunting trips, the Inuit built temporary shelters made of snow blocks, commonly called igloos. The basic igloo design was developed hundreds of years ago. It kept the hunters warm, even in the harshest arctic storm.

CHEERFUL GLOW
An igloo near Thule, Greenland, is lit up by a primus stove. The light inside reveals the spiraling shape of the blocks of ice used to make the igloo. Snow crystals in the walls scatter the light, and the whole room is bathed in the glow. In the Inuit language, "iglu" is actually a word to describe any type of house. A shelter such as this one is called an igluigaq.

BUILDING AN IGLOO
An Inuk (an Inuit man) builds an igloo, using a long ice knife to cut large blocks of tightly packed snow. First, he lays a ring of ice blocks to make a circle up to $3^1/_2$ yards in diameter. Then, some of the blocks are cut to make them slope. As new blocks are added, the walls of the igloo begin to lean inward, forming a dome-shaped igloo. This method is exactly the same as the one used by his ancestors centuries ago.

MAKE A MODEL IGLOO
You will need: self-drying clay, rolling pin, cutting board, ruler, modeling tool, scissors, thick card (8 x 8 in.), pencil, water bowl, white paint, paint brush.

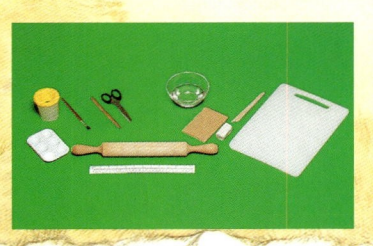

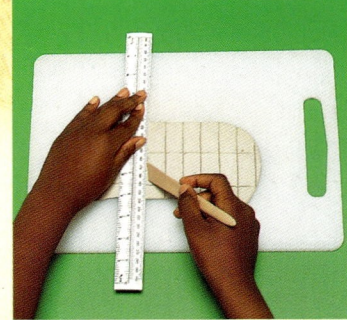

1 Roll out the self-drying clay. It should be around $3/_8$-in. thick. Cut out 30 blocks of clay; 24 must be $3/_4$ x $1^1/_2$ in., and the other 6 must be $1/_2$ x $3/_4$ in.

2 Cut out some card to make an irregular shape. Roll out more clay. Put the template on the clay, and cut around it to make the base of the igloo.

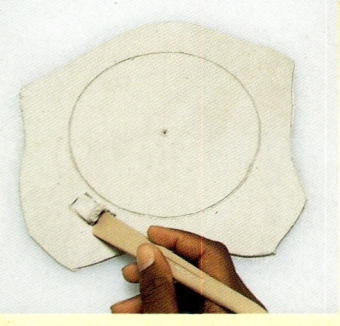

3 Mark a circle with a diameter of $4^3/_4$ in. Cut out a small rectangle on the edge of the circle ($3/_4$ x $1^1/_2$ in.) to make the entrance to the igloo.

50   THE ARCTIC 10,000 B.C.–PRESENT

IGLOO VILLAGE
This engraving, made in 1871, shows a large Inuit village in the Canadian Arctic. Most Inuit igloos were simple, domelike structures. The Inuit built these temporary shelters during their winter hunting trips.

A COZY HOME
An Inuit hunter shelters inside his igloo. A small entrance tunnel prevents cold winds from entering the shelter and traps warm air inside. Outside, the temperature may be as low as -158°F. Inside, the heat from the stove, candles, and the warmth of the hunter's body keeps the air at around 41°F.

THE FINAL BLOCK
An Inuit hunter carefully places the final block of ice on the roof of his igloo. Ancient hunters used sharp ice knives to shape the blocks so that they fitted together exactly. Any gaps were sealed with snow, to prevent the icy winds from entering the shelter.

Inuit hunters built temporary shelters by fitting ice blocks together to form a spiraling dome structure called an igloo. Only hard-packed snow was used to make the building blocks.

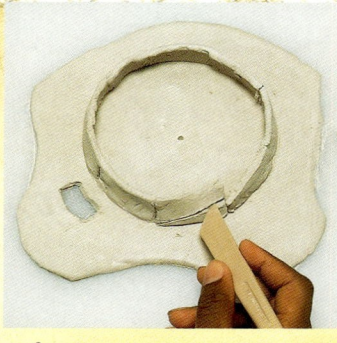

4 Stick nine large blocks around the edge of the circle. Use water to make the clay stick to the base. Cut across two rectangular blocks as shown above.

5 Using your modeling tool, carefully cut a small piece of clay from the corner of each of the remaining blocks, as shown above.

6 Starting from the two blocks cut earlier, build up the walls, slanting each block in as you go. Use the six small blocks at the top. Leave a hole at the top.

7 Use the modeling tool to form a small entrance to the igloo behind the rectangle already cut into the base. When the clay has dried, paint the igloo white.

ARCTIC SEASONAL CAMPS 51

Arctic Children

MODEL IGLOO
An Inuit toddler plays with a model igloo at a nursery in the Canadian Arctic. The blocks of wood spiral upward in the same way as the blocks of ice do in a real igloo, so the toy helps modern children to learn the ancient art of building igloos.

CHILDREN WERE AT THE CENTER of most arctic societies. Inuit babies and younger children spent most of their time riding on their mother's back, nestled in a snug pouch called an amaut. The babies of many arctic groups were named for a respected member of the community, and their birth was celebrated with a huge feast. As children grew older, other members of the family helped the mother to bring up her child.

Today, most arctic children go to school when they are young. However, the children of past generations traveled with their parents as the group moved to fresh reindeer pastures or new hunting grounds. Very young boys and girls were treated equally. As they grew up, however, children helped with different tasks and learned the skills that they would need later on in life. Boys learned how to hunt and tend animals. Girls learned to sew and cook, and to work with animal skins.

BIRTHDAY FEAST
Traditional food is prepared at the birthday celebration of the young boy sitting at the table. Parents often named their newborn babies after people who had been respected in the community, such as a great hunter. The baby was thought to inherit that person's skills and personality.

FEEDING BIRDS TOY
You will need: self-drying clay, rolling pin, ruler, modeling tool, board, two toothpicks, white and brown paint, water pot, paint brush.

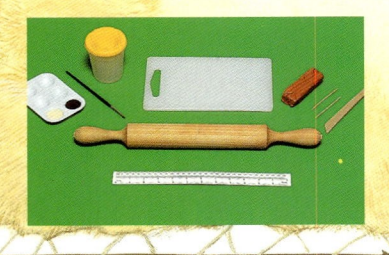

1. Roll out some of the clay into a 8 3/4 x 5 1/2 in. rectangle with a thickness of around 1/2 in. Cut out two large paddles (7 x 1 1/4 in.) and two stalks (1 1/2 x 3/4 in.)

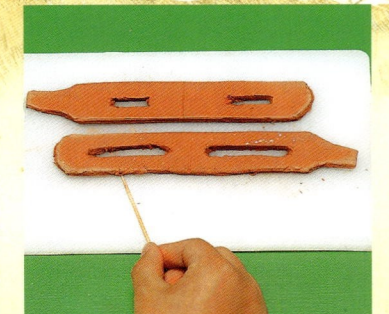

2. Cut two slots on paddle 1 (2 x 3/8 in.) and two on paddle 2 (1 x 3/8 in.). Use a toothpick to pierce a hole in the side of paddle 1 through these slots.

3. Roll out two egg shapes, each about 2 x 1 1/4 in., in the palm of your hands. Make two bird heads and stick them to the egg-shaped bodies.

THE ARCTIC 10,000 B.C.–PRESENT

LENDING A HAND
A Nenet boy and his younger brother help to feed a reindeer calf that has lost its mother. Fathers taught their sons to handle animals from a very early age. Children were encouraged to care for the family's tame deer and dogs.

RIDING HIGH
One of the children in this old illustration is being carried in a special hood, called an amaut, high on the back of his mother's jacket. The second child is tucked inside her mother's sealskin boots. However, it was less common for a child to be carried in this way.

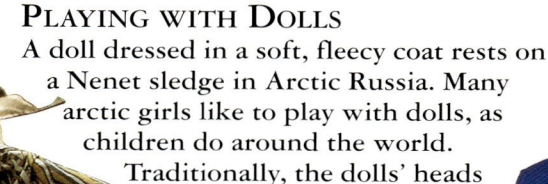

PLAYING WITH DOLLS
A doll dressed in a soft, fleecy coat rests on a Nenet sledge in Arctic Russia. Many arctic girls like to play with dolls, as children do around the world. Traditionally, the dolls' heads were carved from ivory. The doll in the picture, however, is made of modern plastic.

Some arctic children had toys with moving parts, such as this model of two birds. Traditionally, the animals were carved from bone and ivory. The child pulled the paddles to make the birds bob up and down.

4 Stick the stalks you made earlier to the base of each bird's body. Using the toothpick, pierce a small hole through the stalk, close to the body.

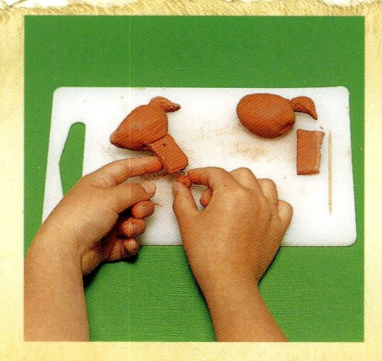

5 Allow the clay bird to dry on its side. You will need to support the stalk with a small piece of clay, to hold the bird upright as it dries.

6 Place the stalk of each bird in the slots in the paddles. Push a toothpick into the holes in the edge of paddle 1, through the stalks and out the other side.

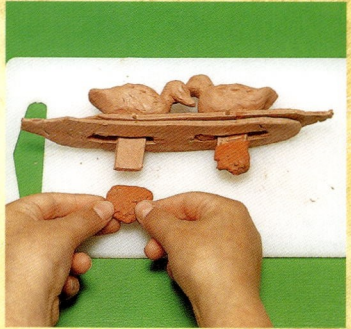

7 Add two small pieces of clay to the bottom of each stalk to keep the birds in place. You can paint the toy once the clay has dried.

ARCTIC CHILDREN

Aztec and Mayan Homes

AZTEC AND MAYAN PEOPLE LIVING in Mesoamerica (known today as Central America) used local materials for building. They had no wheeled transportation, so carrying building materials long distances was very difficult. Stone was the most expensive and longest-lasting building material. It was used for religious buildings, rulers' palaces, and tombs. The homes of ordinary people were built more quickly from cheaper materials, such as sun-dried mud bricks, called adobe, or mud smeared over a framework of wooden poles.

All Mesoamerican homes were very simply furnished. There were no chairs or tables, curtains or carpets—just some jars and baskets for storage and a few reed mats. Everyone, from rulers to slaves, sat and slept on mats on the floor. Most ordinary Aztec homes were L-shaped or built around a courtyard, with a separate bathroom for washing and a small shrine to the gods in the main room.

FAMILY HOME
This present-day Mayan family home is built in traditional style, with red-painted, mud and timber walls. It has one door and no windows. The floor is made of pounded earth. The roof, thatched with dried grass, is steeply sloped, so that the rain runs off it.

BURIED UNDERGROUND
Archaeologists have discovered these remains of houses at the Mayan city of Copan. The roofs, walls and doors have rotted away, but we can still see the stone foundations, used to strengthen the walls. The houses are small and tightly packed together.

MAKE A MAYA HOUSE

You will need: thick card, pencil, ruler, scissors, glue, masking tape, terra-cotta plaster paste (or thin plaster, colored with paint), balsa wood strips, water pot, wide gummed paper tape, brush, short pieces of straw.

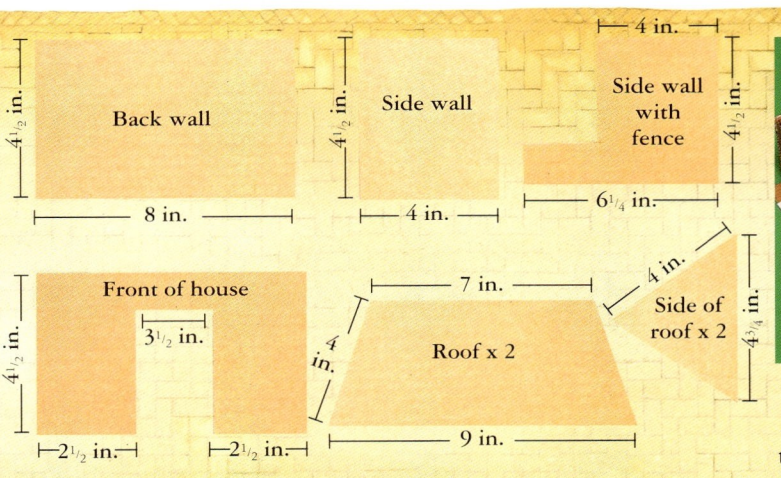

Draw the shapes of the roof and walls of the house on thick card, using the measurements shown. (Please note that the templates are not shown to scale.) Cut out the pieces.

1 Cut out a rectangle 10 x 6 in. from thick card for the base. Stick the house walls and base together with glue. Use masking tape for support.

54 AZTEC & MAYA 2000 B.C.–A.D. 1600

STONEMASONS AT WORK
Mesoamerican masons constructed massive buildings using very simple equipment. Their wedges were made from wood, and their mallets and hammers were shaped from hard volcanic stone. Until around A.D. 900, metal tools were unknown. Fine details were added by polishing stonework with wet sand.

PLASTER
Big stone buildings, such as temples, were often covered with a kind of plaster called stucco. This was then painted with ornate designs. Plaster was made by burning limestone and mixing it with water and colored earth. By the 1400s, there was so much new building in Tenochtitlan, that the surrounding lake became polluted with chemicals from the plastermaking.

plaster *limestone*

SKILLFUL STONEWORK
This carved stone panel from the Mayan city of Chichen-Itza is decorated with a pattern of crosses. It was used to provide a fine facing to thick walls made of rubble and rough stone. This wall decorates a palace building.

A Mayan house provided a cool shelter from the very hot Mexican sun, in addition to keeping out the rain.

2 Paint the walls and base with plaster paste. This will make them look like sun-dried mud. You could also decorate the doorway with balsa wood strips.

3 Put the house on one side to dry. Take your roof pieces and stick them together with glue. Use masking tape to support the roof, as shown.

4 Moisten the wide paper tape and use it to cover the joints between the roof pieces. There should be no gaps. Then cover the whole roof with glue.

5 Press pieces of straw into the glue on the roof. Work in layers, starting at the bottom. Overlap the layers. Attach the roof to the house using glue.

AZTEC AND MAYAN HOMES

Mesoamerican Families

Families were very important to the Maya and Aztecs. By working together, family members provided themselves with food, jobs, companionship, and a home. Each member of a family had special responsibilities. Men produced food or earned the money to buy it. Women cared for babies and the home. From the age of about five or six, children were expected to do their share of the family's work by helping their parents. Because family life was so important, marriages were often arranged by a young couple's parents, or by a matchmaker. The role of matchmaker would be played by an old woman who knew both families well. Boys and girls got married when they were between 16 and 20 years old. The young couple usually lived in the boy's parents' home.

Aztec families belonged to local clan groups, known as calpulli. Each calpulli chose its own leader, collected its own taxes, and built its own temple. It offered help to needy families, but also kept a close eye on how members behaved. If someone broke the law, the whole clan might be punished for that person's actions.

MOTHER AND SON
These Mayan clay figures may show a mother and her son. Boys from noble families went to school at about 15. They learned reading, writing, math, astronomy, and religion.

PAINFUL PUNISHMENT
This codex painting shows a father holding his son over a fire of burning chilies as a punishment. Aztec parents used severe punishments in an attempt to make their children honest and obedient members of society.

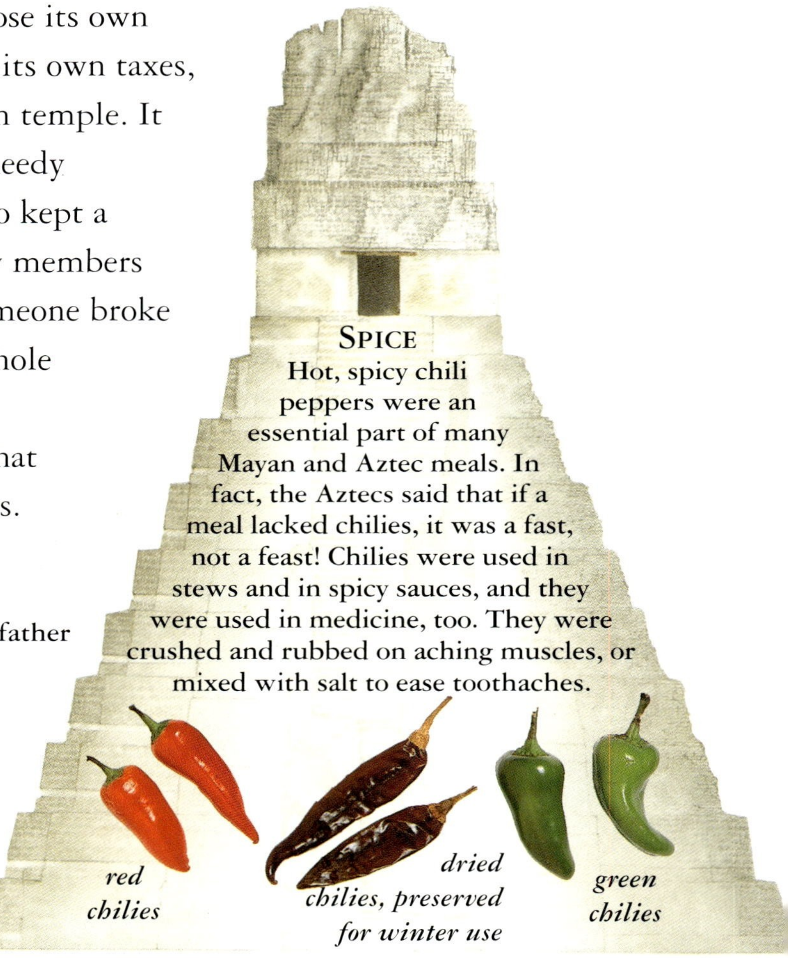

SPICE
Hot, spicy chili peppers were an essential part of many Mayan and Aztec meals. In fact, the Aztecs said that if a meal lacked chilies, it was a fast, not a feast! Chilies were used in stews and in spicy sauces, and they were used in medicine, too. They were crushed and rubbed on aching muscles, or mixed with salt to ease toothaches.

red chilies

dried chilies, preserved for winter use

green chilies

56 AZTEC & MAYA 2000 B.C.–A.D. 1600

IXTILTON
This Aztec mask is made from a black volcanic stone called obsidian. It shows the god Ixtilton, the helper of Huitzilopochtli, the Aztecs' special tribal god. Aztec legends told how Ixtilton could bring darkness and peaceful sleep to tired children.

HUSBAND AND WIFE
The bride and groom in this codex picture of an Aztec wedding have their clothes tied together. This shows that their lives are now joined. Aztec weddings were celebrated with presents and feasting. Guests carried bunches of flowers, and the bride wore special make-up, with her cheeks painted yellow or red. During the ceremony, the bride and groom sat side by side on a mat in front of the fire.

GUARDIAN GODDESS
The goddess Tlazolteotl is shown in this codex picture. She was the goddess of lust and sin. Tlazolteotl was also said to watch over mothers and young children. Childbirth was the most dangerous time in a woman's life, and women who died in childbirth were honored like brave soldiers.

LEARNING FOR LIFE
A mother teaches her young daughter to cook in this picture from an Aztec codex. The girl is making tortillas, which are flat corn (maize) pancakes. You can see her grinding the corn in a metate (grinding stone) using a mano (stone used with the metate). Aztec mothers and fathers trained their children in all the skills they would need to survive in adult life. Children from the families of expert craftspeople usually learned their parents' special skills.

MESOAMERICAN FAMILIES 57

An Incan House

THE INCAS BEGAN AS A SMALL TRIBE living in the Andes mountains of Peru in South America. Like the Aztec and Maya, the Incas preferred to build their homes from stone. White granite was the best, since it is very hard. The roof of each house was pitched at a very steep angle, so that heavy mountain rains could drain off quickly. Timber roof beams were lashed to stone pegs on the gables, and supported by a wooden frame. This was thatched with a tough grass called ichu.

Most houses had just one story, but a few had two or three, joined by rope ladders inside the house, or by stone blocks set into the outside wall. Most had a single doorway that was hung with cloth or hide.

Each building was home to a single family and formed part of a compound. As many as half a dozen houses would be grouped around a shared courtyard. All the buildings belonged to families who were members of the same ayllu, or clan.

MUD AND THATCH
Various types of houses were to be seen in different parts of the Inca Empire. Many were built in old-fashioned and regional styles. These round and rectangular houses in Bolivia are made of mud bricks (adobe). The houses are thatched with ichu grass.

FLOATING HOMES
These houses are built by the Uru people, who fish in Lake Titicaca, in the southern part of Peru, and hunt in the surrounding marshes. They live on the lake shore and also on floating islands made of matted totora reeds. Their houses are made of totora and ichu grass. Both these materials would have been used in the Titicaca area in Incan times. The reeds are collected from the shallows and piled on the floor of the lake. New reeds are constantly added.

upper story

inside hearth

courtyard

PICTURES AND POTTERY
Houses with pitched roofs and windows appear as part of the decoration on this pottery from Pacheco, Nazca, in Peru. To find out about houses in ancient Peru, historians look at surviving towns and ruins, at housing styles still in use today and at old pictures and designs on objects.

SQUARE STONE, ROUND PEG
Squared-off blocks of stone are called ashlars. These white granite ashlars make up a wall in the Incan town of Pisaq. They are topped by a round stone peg. Pegs like these were probably used to support roof beams or other structures, such as ladders from one story to another.

BUILDING MATERIALS
The materials used to build an Incan house depended on local supplies. Rock was the favorite material. White granite, dark basalt, and limestone were used whenever it was possible. Away from the mountains, clay was made into bricks and dried hard in the sun to make adobe. Roof beams were formed from timber poles. Thatch was made of grass or reed.

clay *white granite*
thatch *timber*

BUILDING TO LAST
The Incas built simple, but solid, dwellings in the mountains. The massive boulders used for temples and fortresses are here replaced by smaller, neatly cut stones. Notice how the roof beams are lashed to the gables to support the thatch. Stone roofs were very rare, even on the grandest houses. Timber joists provide an upper story. The courtyard is used just as much as the inside of the house for everyday living.

Married Life in Incan Times

WEDDINGS WERE SOME of the happiest occasions in an Incan village. They offered a chance for the whole community to take time off of work. The day was celebrated with dancing, music, and feasting. The groom would probably be 25 years of age, at which point he was regarded as an adult citizen, and his bride would be a little younger—about 20.

For the first year of the marriage, a couple did not have to pay any taxes, either in goods or labor. However, most of their lives would be spent working hard. When they were elderly, they would still be expected to help with household chores. Even later, when they became too old or sick to take care of themselves, they received free food and clothes from the State warehouse. They would then be cared for by their clan or family group.

Not everyone was expected to get married. The mamakuna (virgins of the sun) lived much like nuns, in a special convent in the Incan town of Cuzco. They wove fine cloth and carried out religious duties. No men were allowed to enter the mamakuna's building.

WEDDING CLOTHES
An Inca nobleman would get married in a very fine tunic. This one is from the southern coast of Peru. Commoners had to wear simpler clothes, but couples were presented with free new clothes from the State warehouses when they married.

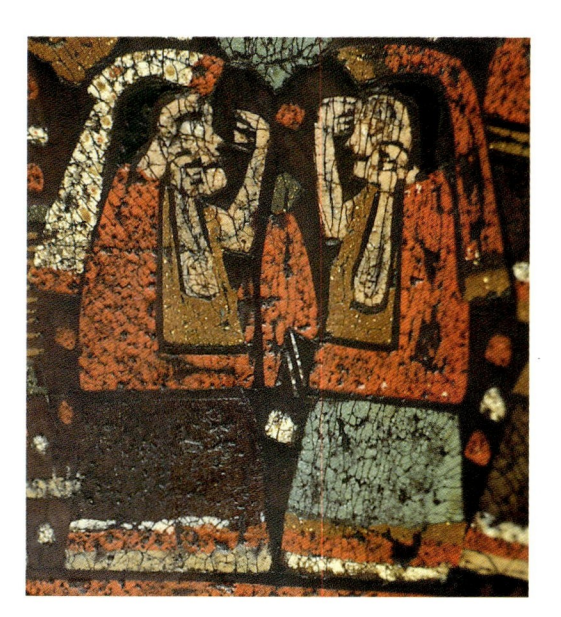

MARRIAGE PROSPECTS
Two Inca noblewomen are painted on the side of this kero (wooden beaker). Women of all social classes were only allowed to marry with the approval of their parents and of State officials. They were expected to remain married for life, and divorce was forbidden. If either the husband or wife was unfaithful, he or she could face trial and might even be put to death.

REAL PEOPLE
This jar is over 1,300 years old. Unlike the portraits on many jars, it seems to show a real person sitting down and thinking about life. It reminds us that ancient cultures and civilizations were made up of individuals who fell in love, raised children, and grew old, just as people do today.

A Royal Marriage

A prince of the emperor's family marries in Cuzco. The scene is imagined by an artist of the 1800s. An emperor had many secondary wives in addition to his sister-empress. Between them, they produced many princes and princesses. Incan royal families were divided by jealousy and by complicated relations, which often resulted in open warfare. The emperor ordered his officials to keep tight control over who married whom. His own security on the throne depended on it.

A Home of their Own

When a couple married, they left their parents' houses and moved into their own home, like this one at Machu Picchu, in the Andes. The couple now took official control of the fields they would work. These had been allocated to the husband when he was born. Most couples stayed in the area occupied by their own clan, so their relatives would remain nearby.

His and Hers

The everyday lives of most married couples in the Inca Empire were taken up by hard work. Men and women were expected to do different jobs. Women made the chicha beer and did the cooking, weaving, and some field work. Men did field work and fulfiled the mit'a labor tax in service to the Inca State. They might build irrigation channels or repair roads.

MARRIED LIFE IN INCAN TIMES 61

Glossary

A
adobe Plaster made from clay and straw, used by Pueblo people of Central America, Egyptians, and Mesopotamians on their homes.
agriculture Farming—the activity of growing crops and breeding animals.
amaut Black pouch used by Inuit people of the north American Arctic to carry babies and young children.
ancestor An individual from whom one is descended, such as a great-great-grandfather.
archaeologist A person who studies ancient remains or ruins.
atrium The hallway or courtyard of a Roman house. The middle of the atrium was open to the sky.
Aztecs Mesoamerican people who lived in northern and central Mexico. They were at their most powerful btween A.D. 1350 and A.D. 1520.

B
banquet A rich, elaborate feast served with great ceremony.
brahmins The priests, members of the first caste in India.
bronze A metal made from a mixture of copper and tin.

C
calpulli An Aztec family or neighborhood group. The calpulli enforced law and order. It arranged education, training, and welfare benefits for its members.
caste One of four social classes into which Hindus in India were divided.
civil servant An official who carries out government administration.
codex An Aztec folding book.
Confucianism The Western name for the teachings of the Chinese philosopher Kong Fuzi (Confucius), which call for social respect for one's family and ancestors.
cremation The burning of dead bodies.

D
dowry Money that is given to a newly married couple, usually by the bride's father.
dynasty A period of rule by the same royal family, such as the pharaohs of Egypt and the rulers in the Chinese empire.

F
faience A type of opaque glass that is often blue or green. It is made from quartz or sand, lime, ash, and natron.
feud A long-standing quarrel, especially between two families.

H
hunter-gatherer A person who lives by hunting animals and gathering wild roots and plants for food.

I
igloo An Inuit word meaning "house," which is often used to refer to Inuit shelters built from ice or snow blocks.
imperial Relating to the rule of an emperor or empress.
Inuit The native people of the North American Arctic, Canada, and Greenland, as distinguished from those of Asia and the Aleutian Islands. Inuit is also the general name for an Eskimo in Canada.

K
kero An Incan drinking vessel.
kimono A loose robe with wide sleeves, worn by both men and women in Japan.

L
longhouse The chief building of a Viking homestead.
loom A wooden frame used for weaving cloth.
lyre A harplike instrument.

M

maki sushi Rolls of vinegared rice made with fish and vegetable fillings.

Maya People who lived in southeastern Mexico, Guatamala, and Belize.

millet A grass-type plant that produces edible seeds.

mosaic A picture made up of many small squares or cubes of glass, stone, or pottery, and set in soft concrete.

mummy A human, or sometimes animal, body preserved by drying.

N

Nenet A reindeer herding people of southern Siberia.

New Kingdom The period of Egyptian history between 1550–1070 B.C.

O

oppida The Roman name for fortified Celtic towns.

P

papyrus A tall reed that grows in the river Nile, used to make a kind of paper by the ancient Egyptians.

paratha A fried wheat bread eaten in northern India.

pharaoh A ruler of ancient Egypt.

prehistoric Belonging to the time before written records were made.

Pueblo People from the southwest of Mexico who lived in villages built of mud and stone.

pyramid A large pointed monument with a broad, square base and four triangular sides.

Q

quern A simple machine, made from two stones, that is used to grind corn.

R

relief A carved stone slab.

S

scribe A professional writer, a clerk, or civil servant.

T

tablet A flat piece of clay of various shapes and sizes, used for writing.

tablinium The formal reception room and study in a Roman house.

taboo A rule or custom linked with shamanic tribal religious beliefs that shows respect to the spirits.

temple A special building used for worshipping a god.

terra-cotta Brown-red earthen ware used for making pots and sculpture.**textile** Any cloth that has been woven, such as silk or cotton.

textile Any cloth that has been woven, such as silk or cotton.

threshing To beat or thrash out grain from corn.

tipi Conical tent with a frame of poles, covered with animal skins, used by the Native North American Plains people.

tribe A group of people who share a common language and way of life.

triclinium The dining room in a Roman house.

V

Viking A member of the Scandinavian peoples who lived by sea-raiding in the early Middle Ages.

W

warrior A man who fights in wars.

wigwam A Native American house made of bark, rushes, or skins, spread over arched poles that were lashed together.

winnowing Separating grains of wheat and rice from their papery outer layer, called chaff.

Index

A
alphabet 29
ancestors 27
Arctic 49-53
Aztec 54-7

B
banquets 14-15, 19, 24
beer 14, 15
bread 14-15, 19
bricks 8, 9, 11, 12, 13, 45, 54, 58
bronze 25
Buddhists 18
building materials 4, 8-9, 11, 12-13, 15, 20, 30, 44, 48, 54, 58, 59
burial graves 41
butchers 25

C
Celts 36-9
childbirth 57
children 5, 10, 22, 23, 26-7, 28, 32, 36, 40, 46-7, 52-3
China 20-5
chums (tents) 48
clans 56, 58
clothes 26, 37, 42, 43, 60
Cnut, King 43
cold-climate homes 48-9
Confucius 22-3

D
decorations 6, 16, 17
desserts 15
diet 18-19
dolls 47, 53
dome-shaped homes 44-5
drink 38
dyes 37

E
earth lodges 45
education 5, 22, 28-9, 34-5, 40, 52, 56
Egypt 12-15
emperors 23, 61

F
faience 14, 15
family life 10-11, 22-3, 26-7, 32-3, 36, 40-1, 46, 56-7
farming 8, 11, 36
fashions 11
feuds 40-1
fights 40-1
fishing 11
flavors 25
floating homes 58
floods 13, 18
food 14-15, 18-19, 24-5, 38-9, 52
foot binding 22
funerals 32, 33

G
games 28-9
gardens 12, 18, 31
good luck charms 7, 17
Greece 28-9

H
Han dynasty 20, 22
harmony 20-1
Hindus 18
household goods 10
hunter-gatherers 8
hunting 38, 39, 46

I
igloos 50-1, 52
Inca Empire 58-61
India 16-19
Inuit tribe 48, 50-1
Ixtilton 57

J
Japan 26-7

K
kitchen god 24
Kong Fuzi (Confucius) 22-3

L
lessons 34-5
locks and keys 30, 36
longhouses 4, 8, 44, 45

M
marriage 22, 26, 32, 33, 42, 46, 56, 57, 60-1
Maya 54-7
meat 24
medicine 27
memorial stones 40, 43
Mesopotamia 10-11
motherhood 10
mud bricks 8, 9, 11, 12, 13, 54, 58
Muslims 18

N
Nile, River 12
noblewomen 22, 23
nomads 5
North American Indians 44-7

O
ovens 9

P
palaces 16
pharaohs 14-15
plaster 55
pottery 9, 10, 37, 59
punishments 56

Q
querns 39

R
rich and poor 16-17
role play 46
Roman Empire 30-5
roof charms 21

S
schooling 5, 22, 28-9, 34-5, 40, 52, 56
seasonal camps 50-1
servants 22
Shang dynasty 24
social class 16
Song dynasty 22
soul houses 13
spices 18, 19, 56
staple foods 18
stone 9, 54, 58, 59
Stone Age 8-9
stonemasons 55

T
tents 44, 48
thatch 20, 44, 54, 58
tipis 44
Tlazolteotl 57
tools 55
totem poles 44
town houses 9, 30
towns 12
toys 27, 28-9, 53

V
vegetarians 18
Vikings 40-3
villages 8-9

W
wealth 5
weaving 37, 43
weddings 22, 32, 33, 42, 57, 60, 61
whale bones 48, 49
wigwams 44
windows 49
wine 14
women 5, 10, 22, 23, 24, 26, 42-3, 60, 61
working together 26-7, 56
writing 34, 35

64 INDEX